# Be My Guest... and pay me!

## Pamela Demorest

## The Arthouse Company, LLC

Published by The Arthouse Company, LLC.


Library of Congress Cataloging-in-Publication Data
Pamela Demorest
Be My Guest...and pay me!

ISBN NUMBER: 978-1484945094

For my parents Jack and Lucille,
and my favorite guys, Kirk, Calvin & Jackson.

# BE MY GUEST...and pay me!

The ultimate guide to earning money from home by renting out your extra living space

LIST OF CHAPTERS

How operating a city vacation rental gave me more time, freedom and usually *pays my mortgage*. Learn the #1 lesson to live by in any business.

*2 crucial* questions to ask yourself before you proceed! The shortest distance between now and making some money. Avoid wasting your time and resources from the start

The key to creating the wow factor! The most popular set ups being used now. Getting your space ready--*5 essential* mistakes to avoid. Details about everything you will *need* to offer, and a few things you might *want* to offer. A great bed is the ultimate comfort zone, so make yours inviting. The pro's and con's of offering a kitchen facility.

The secret to creating a *4 star bathroom* on a budget. No matter what your set up--comfort and privacy equal luxury. Why you should never use keys for your rental!

## 4) Cleanliness *REALLY* is next to Godliness

A lack of cleanliness is a deal breaker for most people! Whether you do the cleaning yourself or have a team working for you, *all maintenance* is crucial. Create a timesaving and detailed cleaning checklist (sample included in the book). The trick for finding the best employee to clean your place and keep them invested in your rental.

## 5) Top-Notch Advertising and Marketing

Embrace the Internet and *score* with a winning formula for success! Deciding where to spend your money and how to invest your time. Craigslist isn't perfect, but it's close! Master the maintenance steps for effective Craigslist ads! The **best** vacation rental web sites to join and why. Bust through the mystery that determines website rankings--and enjoy the secret of online success-- with this proven and streamlined *lesson.* Learn effective promotional ideas to bump up your business year round. Setting your price point to be attractive, reasonable and competitive. The power of social media networking!

Customer service is what hooks them! Save your precious time using form letters-- (8 included). How to gracefully handle property showings and delicate booking situations. Setting critical policy for deposits, taxes and cleaning fees. Which payment methods to consider, and why you should *never-- ever* accept cash. The *Number 1* reason why you must get paid in full before your guests ever arrive.

7) **The Rental Agreement: The holy grail of protection for yourself and guests** Page 125

*The most significant* document needed in running a vacation rental (rental agreement template included). Explain what you offer and all restrictions of your property. How to gently spell out guest conduct from parties to pets. The subtle warning of extra fees for damages or excessive cleaning needs. How to ensure that guests feel more secure by protecting all parties involved. The vital issues regarding insurance, business licenses, occupancy limitations and taxes.

8) **A couple of almost horror stories and what not to do** Page 141

Learn how to avoid the *top 4* most costly mistakes you can make. How to avoid the dreaded removal of a guest --I've only had to do this once in six years--and it was *my* mistake!

Are you ready? What are the guests' first impression of you and your place?

Become invaluable to your guests—even from a distance. How much of your time should you spend with guests? How to follow up after guests leave and insure you are their number one choice for future visits and referrals. Keeping in touch with these great people you will meet. The hidden secrets of promoting your rental.

## RESOURCES

Craigslist, Ikea, HomeAway.com, airbnb.com, rentalmadeeasy.com, rentalspot.com, rentalo.com, villa4vacation.com, vrbo.com, 1villa.net, flipkey.com, vacationrentaldirect.com, OMGtravel.org, James Wolf Insurance, Wordpress, Google, Bed Bath & Beyond, Anna's Linens, Costco, Facebook, Coffee Wholesale USA, rentalcalendarsdirect.com, elance.com, squareup.com.

# Introduction

## How a city vacation rental gave me more time, freedom and usually pays my mortgage!

---

*"Do what you do so well that they will want to see it again and bring their friends."* - WALT DISNEY

---

Below are just a few of the numerous guest reviews (too many to list) on my web site from happy customers who have stayed over the past few years at my popular *city vacation rental*.

*Excellent! Everything was perfect! Thank you, we'll be back!*

Catherine & Joseph - Phoenix, AZ

*Spending 3 weeks in LA with The Bungalow as my own special nest and place of retreat has been wonderful. You have done everything to make your guests feel comfortable and pampered, and it really felt like coming home each evening rather than returning to a hotel room. I hope to return again on another visit to LA.*

Rachel - London, UK

*My mother and I were in California visiting family and thought that the bungalow would be a great place to stay. We were right!! We were close enough to Glendale and Burbank but also not too far from the sights of Hollywood and Sunset. The area is very quiet and peaceful and it was so nice to stay in a relaxing atmosphere vs. a busy, large hotel. We loved the local restaurants and the Whole Foods right across the street. We will absolutely tell our friends and family to stay at the bungalow when they head out to California. Hopefully we will be able to stay at the bungalow sooner than later. Thanks so much.*

Helene - Pittsburgh, PA

*We had a great time at this bungalow. It was perfect! During our 2-week stay in CA we stayed in 3 different rentals from Home Away & we liked this one the best. Perfect location, perfect size, & all the perfect little touches! We will be back:) The owners thought of everything! Extra pillows in the closet, nice shampoos & soaps in the bathroom, plenty of cups, bowls & silverware. I loved the shower! The place was spotless & very quiet. When you came back in the evening it just felt so comfy & relaxing.*
*This place is a gem!*

Sabrina - Brevard, NC

*I decided on this guest bungalow, as my place of surgery recovery for a few days and could not have made a better decision. I wanted a place that was comfortable and quiet, yet conveniently close to everything. Pamela, the owner, is very responsive, and paid extra attention to this place to give her guests all the amenities that a guest could ask for - the most comfortable bed with down comforter, A/C, two (!) heaters, desk and loveseat area, strong Wi-Fi signal, cable TV, nice bath area with full-size shampoo/conditioner, body wash and lotion, sink with sponge and dish-wash soap, fridge, microwave, bowls, plates, cups, mugs, condiments, coffeemaker with delicious (!) coffee, hot water brewer with tea bags... need I say more? Oh yeah, came back a few weeks later for another stay, and will be coming back again. Perfect, Perfect, Perfect!*

Renee - Orange County, CA

*A very nice and perfect clean place! It had everything we needed for our stay. I would recommend it to everyone. Everything was well maintained and Pamela was always a big help and responded every time so quick. The neighbourhood is nice as well, mostly residential and we felt safe there. Keep in mind that a car is best to go from the bungalow to any other places and around in the city (it's already written in the listing). We will definitely come back! Great Place!*

Fabian - Dijon, France

Our guests have come from as far away as Germany, Israel, France, Australia, England, Spain, throughout the United States, and a few from just a couple of blocks away. Whether they are staying for one night, or two months, I have found these travelers to be wonderful people who not only enjoy, but also are **grateful** for a unique alternative to hotel/motel lodging. Most important is the fact that renting space to these guests **OFTEN PAYS MY MORTGAGE**, and has done so for over the past six years!

Since you are reading this book, you no doubt are attracted to the idea of making additional income from home. It might surprise you to know that not only is it relatively easy, but also can be lucrative to create a *city vacation rental,* right from where you are -- now.

By converting some little-used space at home into a vacation rental, I have made **thousands of dollars** right in my own backyard! Which is pretty ironic, since I was looking everywhere else for extra money, except in my own yard. The whole *Wizard of Oz* concept of already having what you need right at home was certainly proven to me.

First let me be very clear that although it's a great set up, you do not need a separate building to make money with a home-based vacation rental. Many people offer rooms in their house for pay. Some people are in a position to rent their primary residence, apartment or house and stay elsewhere—while traveler's pay to stay at their place. There are several possible scenarios outlined in this book.

The vacation rental industry is an annual twenty-four-billion-dollar business [1]. This figure doesn't even include business travelers, yet that demographic often finds their way to city vacation rentals. These types of city rentals are an increasingly popular alternative to hotel lodging, providing economy and escape from of the unwanted trappings of a hotel, without compromising comfort or safety. You could be part of this growing industry without the overhead of most businesses.

Today's vacation rentals are not limited to "destination" locations, as many people believe. A successful vacation rental does not have to be a second property located in a far-off exotic location, like a beach house in Maui, or log cabin at the highest peak of Telluride. Remote rentals are certainly abundant and have their place, but they're often seasonal, and travel to them is expensive.

Second property destination rentals have taken a big hit from the recent decline in the global economy [2]. Many travel agency owners believe the current economic distress is giving luxury travel a bad name—for both the very wealthy and the average Joe. That's where you come in because more travelers are vacationing in well-known cities, which offer a broad variety of activities and attractions, at a better value. My vacation rental is in Los Angeles, *near a freeway*, and is booked almost constantly!

If you want proof of how much money is spent on vacation

---

[1] According to "Poised for Change" an article in PhoCusWright's 2008 report representing the first comprehensive sizing and analysis of the vacation rental market.

[2] Reported in Jayne Clark's article " Guilt trip: Luxury travelers tone it down in hard times" featured in USA Today March 6, 2009.

rentals, consider the fact that in 2010 and 2011, while the whole world was suffering a financial meltdown, the popular website Homeaway.com, which advertises vacation rentals, paid for Superbowl ads to promote their business! Superbowl ads are *the* most expensive ads on television. Another very popular online vacation rental site, airbnb.com, exploded on the scene and was reported by the Wall Street Journal in 2011 to have secured a BILLION dollar valuation. These sources are great for advertising your rental, but you can begin now *without* putting money out for their fees. Or you can utilize their services along with your own marketing efforts.

This guide provides simple instructions for setting up, marketing and managing a successful, *virtually automatic* city vacation rental. What do I mean by automatic? Once the set up and easy marketing and operation strategies have been put into place, there is very little time or effort required to attracting superior customers and earning consistent income from a city vacation rental.

Offered here are all the details required to operate a robust vacation rental, from protecting yourself from liability, to the reasons why you should never put fresh flowers on a table, or provide a bar of soap in the bathroom (soap bars are unsanitary and costly), and everything in between.

If you happen to already have a vacation rental with a second home, or destination rental that's great! This book can help you learn to self manage that rental avoiding or minimizing the cost of a third party management company. Self-management is not only more profitable; the fact is that no third party will ever *care* as much about your property as you do, so why would you pay someone else to manage it?

Although, some travelers will always prefer a hotel they have experienced and trusted, an astonishing number of people seek autonomy from a hotel staff, or the invasive corporate and leisure groups so often encountered in hotels. Not to mention, everyone seems to be shopping for deals these days.

And these same travelers often want *comforts that feel like home* when on the road. One reason Bed & Breakfasts are so successful is because they provide touches of home or privacy that just can't be found in a hotel. That feeling of a home away from home is yet another benefit of a personalized city vacation rental.

If you can create a space for lodging that is truly special and unique, travelers will be very willing to pay to stay there. If those guests are made to feel special and *save money*, they will come back time and again.

With the help of this book, those people can find **your** rental.

# Chapter 1

## My Story

---

*"Success doesn't come to you…you to to it."*- MARVA COLLINS

---

Several years ago my husband's television editing job went on hiatus, our son was just four years old, and I needed a way to supplement our income without leaving my nest. We had so much financial stress I often forgot my name—or at least wanted to. My in-laws gifted us airline tickets to Canada along with the offer to watch our son, urging us to take a little break.

My husband convinced me that this was an opportunity to go away and rethink some things. I personally have a hard time "rethinking" anything when I'm worried about money, but like I said before, the offer was too perfect to pass up, so we went for it, despite our rapidly shrinking savings account.

Next came the task of finding a place to stay that would be comfortable, located near the activities of the city and … really cheap! We struck out with any brand name hotel as those prices were way out of our budget. And just as we were actually considering going the route of hostels (which can be fun when you're a teenager but seems a bit spartan as a grown up), we decided to check out Craigslist to see if there might be some small, unknown, charming little hotel that the world hadn't yet discovered. There wasn't.

But…what really jumped off that list were *city vacation rentals!* Who even knew those existed? Not us, but apparently some other people did because there were so many listings, I was glued to the computer! I searched other cities (maybe this was just a Canadian thing?) including my own and yep…we had them in Los Angeles too. So did San Francisco, New York, Seattle, you get the picture.

There were listings *in the city* for rooms in people's houses, guest cottages, converted garages, entire apartments, studio's and lofts that could all be rented <u>short term</u>. I had only thought of vacation rentals as being far off or exotic locations. Maybe you have too?

Craigslist had numerous alternatives to the standard fare of an all too expensive hotel, a questionable motel, or a quaint little Bed and Breakfast (B&B) that might be full of cat hair, cigarette smoke and dust! (Really, I experienced all three in one place).

I am not knocking all B&B's, but we were still reeling from the experience at the above mentioned very dirty B&B that turned into a a real hassle with a year long credit card dispute. Besides that, not everyone is interested in making small talk with strangers in a forced communal space with a set menu! I personally prefer some anonymity over "old charm", but that's just me.

I don't mean to imply you are a novice with Internet searching, and you probably already know how great Craigslist is, but to see so many places for lodging listed that were actually, for the most part cheap, was a huge surprise to me! Not cheap as in dingy motel cheap, but cheap compared to the higher end hotels that we wish we could have afforded.

We focused in on a place that looked to be the little oasis that might help me to forget my worries. Located in the best part of Vancouver, it was a really great looking place nestled off of a private courtyard. It had it's own entrance, a small but seemingly efficient kitchen (we could eat in and not have to spend so much at restaurants), a great looking bedroom and a really great looking bathtub, where I could see myself soaking up some much needed down time!

I dreamed of quiet...no one running down the halls late at night (which I have experienced even at high end hotels), no dangerous neighborhood to navigate on the outskirts of town in a strange city, no smoking room nearby where dreaded noxious fumes might find their way to us, no car alarms going off in the parking lot that our room would inevitably be next to should we book at your basic motel near a freeway for the same price!

The only problem we could see with this place was that they required a MINIMUM four night stay, but we could only stay three. The availability calendar shown for this rental was completely empty for two weeks, so we decided that whoever owned the place would probably be happy to have us for three days instead of no booking at all.

So my husband called the owner. After explaining we were coming to town and wanted to stay in his vacation rental, but couldn't stay the required four nights, the guy on the other end of the line went into some uppity tirade about how great the place was, what a first rate location it was, how it's always booked, and **"NO"** we couldn't just come for three nights unless we wanted to pay for four! My husband pointed out that the calendar was completely open and asked if it wasn't better to have some kind of booking that week instead of nothing... and the guy rudely dismissed him with **"NO"** and then hung up the phone!

Well that was a little slap in the face! It was shocking that anybody advertising any kind of a business at all could be so rude, unprofessional, and so completely devoid of customer service. How does he know we wouldn't actually have paid the full four nights—had he at least been courteous on the phone, because it still would have been cheaper than a hotel?

That man not only lost out on our business for our first trip to Vancouver, he lost out on much more. Had he been open, flexible, had a shred of decency, or even a good explanation of why our request wouldn't work for him, we probably would have stayed anyway — and— had it been a nice place...would have told *everyone* we know about this great little place to stay in Vancouver.

He missed out on the potential to cross link into what was to be our future business by building a relationship with us. I am crosslinked with other vacation rental operators and we sometime share referrals. We also could have been his repeat customers, because we ended up loving Vancouver and will go back. He lost out on the kind of advertising you cannot buy...*a great personal experience that people can't wait to pass on to others.* I get a herd of new people each year who learn about my place by a friend or family member who have stayed at my rental at some point in time.

**LESSON #1** – be nice to *everyone* who calls or emails asking about your rental, always! There are too many competitors for potential guests to turn to. You will not be the only game in town, but you can be one of the best. This concept is true for any business.

Back to our pending trip…I decided that since our first call put us in touch with someone who might just be a psycho, there was probably something wrong with each place listed... strange smells, loud animals, unexplainable shadows, creaking doors.

We ended up booking into a hotel after all. Not high end, not low end. It was right in the middle. We would still have to use our credit card again for an amount higher than what we hoped for, adding to the balance that we were desperately trying to pay off.

So off we went to Vancouver to a predictable mid range hotel. We got the typical Queen bed with a generic dark floral scratchy bedspread, one small corner round table with two chairs sitting on a worn carpet, a small media cabinet with a standard TV, two small bedside tables with very boring overly bright bolted down lamps that can't be adjusted, and one Gideon's Bible. No offense to anyone, but why not include some non religious reading materials as well, if you are including any at all?

No little kitchenette where I might keep snacks handy. In fact, there was no counter space of any kind besides the small round table in the corner. The small bathroom had the usual tiny bottle of bad shampoo, no hair conditioner, an extremely harsh little bar of soap, two thin little towels, and a little rickety hair dryer bolted to the wall.

Okay...we all know these places. They are a cookie cutter duplicate of every other room with a queen bed that a low to mid range hotel could offer. An okay place to sleep, but nothing special while you're awake! Special usually costs a lot more.

After settling in, we headed out to explore. Walking down the hall, we had to dodge an awkwardly large cleaning cart while listening to the cleaning people talking a bit loudly as we passed a few open doors. At least most high end hotels have an appearance of real discretion about maintenance, but most lower priced places don't seem to care what guests observe.

Making our way to the elevator next to the standard loud ice machine, we found ourselves back in the dingy lobby, where we passed a crowd of tourists, all waiting in line for a bell man. The front desk agent was pretty frazzled trying to manage three guests at once, so we realized it wasn't a good time to ask for extra towels.

At dinner that night we started to rehash the whole vacation rental phone call from the jerk who was so rude. We talked about what a great idea a vacation rental in the city was, and how we wished we weren't checked into just another boring hotel, and then... *all at...once the lightbulb went off in my head.* Our small guesthouse at home was being used as nothing more than a glorified storage closet! It had a great shower in it, but we rarely used the space at all!

24

As someone not fond of math, I usually stay far away from numbers, but I mentally started adding. The guy in Vancouver was asking about $100 U.S. dollars a day. Let's see... thirty days in a month x $100 = $3,000. And even if we decided to rent our guest-house to a full time tenant instead of vacationers, we could never ask for that kind of rent.

Wow, this was good! But of course I couldn't assume we could get people to stay 30 days a month, or could I? Besides that, I wondered how the heck do you even get started? But the potential of making that kind of money was very enticing. That amount would cover our mortgage and more. What if we somehow could turn that extra space into a short-term vacation rental? I came home from that trip with my imagination pretty revved up.

After spending a few days researching the vacation rental industry, I was convinced this was a viable home business, but I was left wondering how the heck do you do this? And what about the risk? I let the paranoid part of my brain entertain all sorts of scenarios. Creeps would lurk about my yard....smokers would stain the paint...squatters would try to scam me... my child might be at risk. Then it occurred to me that my husband and I almost rented such a place and we are not creeps, smokers, or squatters! We are clean respectable people who can appreciate a deal!

My method for screening people with the rental agreement, along with secure payment practices, will protect you. People looking to practice any kind of "shady" dealings, usually don't want to sign a document agreeing to the conditions contained in my rental agreement (included for you in Chapter 7. And they certainly don't want to be as visible as people renting vacation rentals in a private home are.

I jumped into my research, put a simple plan of action together, set up my vacation rental and hoped for the best. And it worked —in fact it worked beautifully. I have earned much more income renting my guesthouse as a *short-term vacation rental*, than I ever could have renting to a permanent tenant. I could make $30 per day from a long-term tenant, versus $100 per day with my vacation rental! Gee, that's a no brainer.

You will also be thrilled to know that you don't have to invest in a secondary property in a distant land for this additional income, like most vacation rental owners. You won't need to deal with real estate agents, financing, new property taxes, or the roller coaster of a property purchase. If you have ever purchased a property, you can no doubt remember how stressful that experience can be. Right?

Unless you are a professional real estate investor, buying a property can be pretty daunting. But how great is it that you can take what you already have right now, where you already live, and create another stream of income?

My rental has provided *instant* income much quicker than any stock or short-term investment I personally would risk rolling the dice on. But then again, I am not much of a gambler. But just like gambling in Vegas, the return on a vacation rental is immediate, without the chance of losing.

In fact, I took a booking in my rental just this week that took me only two minutes but paid me $665.00. This was possible because the booking was for returning guests, and much of the process to secure their reservation was already on file in my office. But this booking really came about because I created an experience they couldn't forget the first time they stayed in my rental. I created a home away from home for them!

Each reservation I book takes an average of only eight minutes or less of my time! From working literally only a few hours last month, I made and EXTRA $2,180.00... the month before, $1,985.00 EXTRA, and next month I am scheduled to make a whopping $2,475.00 in EXTRA income! That is an amazing average of $24,000.00 annually from a single tiny unit. And that's without ever leaving my house!

I know millions of people in these hard economic times are working two or in some cases three jobs, just to make their monthly nut! I have much more time and freedom in my life running this business than I could ever have working for someone else, that is for sure.

It's a major benefit of my vacation rental business to be my own boss. I love not having to be accountable to anyone else, or working strange hours on top of my regular job for some extra income. I don't have to submit to some grueling odd job like toiling long into the night stuffing envelopes, telephone sales, or begging my friends to sign up for some new miracle in a multi-level marketing "opportunity", just to make some extra cash. I don't have to invest in training materials whose price exceeds any profits I could ever make from selling cleaning supplies and shampoos to everyone I've ever met. I don't have to spend one minute or penny on someone else's vision.

And knowing what I know now, if my guesthouse didn't already exist, I would happily invest in and endure construction to build one, or convert my garage into a cozy vacation rental. Any investment that one can make to create such a space would pay for itself in time, increase the value the home, and be very beneficial during a sale of that property.

My plan of action makes management and maintenance so seamless that I currently run my busy vacation rental remotely from my primary home 420 miles away! All without a third party manager! In fact, our move from Los Angeles to the West Sonoma countryside in Northern California was for the most part, subsidized with our vacation rental income. That income continues to flow and *usually pays my mortgage!*

**Be My Guest...and pay me!** is the guide I wish I had when I started my vacation rental business. Let's get started!

# CHAPTER 2

## Your Story

---

*"The difference between a mountain and a molehill is your perspective."*- AL NEUHARTH

---

You will be happy to know that a down economy is a great time to start up a city vacation rental! I began my rental when the economy was in great shape several years ago. It was a time when banks were freely lending money to people for houses they couldn't afford, but that is another book for sure. Our rental was busy then (once we mastered the crucial marketing steps outlined in this book) but... we continue to be even busier now as people are seeking better value in today's shaky economy.

Whether you want to cushion your nest egg, get your kid braces, pay for college, save yourself from foreclosure, plan a remodel, pay your mortgage, go shopping for Italian boots, or buy an electric car... you will be amazed at how the dollars add up with a steady stream of people staying in your city vacation rental.

***There are 2 crucial*** questions to ask yourself before you proceed!

1) Realistically, where is the best space for your rental? If you have a separate unit, great— this might be easier than you think. If you are considering using a room in your house, are having guests in your house something you can live with? Have you discussed this with your family members? Can you all work together toward the common goal of making money. Can you create a situation where everyone is comfortable?

Although having a guesthouse or a detached unit is ideal in my opinion, you don't *need* a separate unit. Elizabeth, a friendly competitor in Los Angeles, lives alone and runs a thriving short-term rental business out of her main house. Her set up is more like a Bed and Breakfast or a boarding house and attracts the type of traveler who enjoys staying in a private home with personal amenities--like home cooked meals. Elizabeth prefers this type of renter to a permanent tenant because she can control her flow of occupancy. She can make money or not, according to her own schedule. Thousands of people all over the world list rooms for rent on the popular airbnb.com website as well as Craigslist.

2) Are you prepared to treat this entire operation as a business? Although you can start simply and slowly, the way to make the most money is to *maintain* the marketing strategies outlined to invite maximum traffic to your place. Once you are set up – maintenance is easy and only requires minimal attention.

Once you are clear with the answers you came up with, the next thing is to decide how soon you will be prepared to have your first guests. You can probably set your space up within a few days, providing you don't have any major work like painting or buying furniture or carpet.

I didn't spend one dime on anything *except* a bed and two matching bedside tables from Ikea when I started. I kept it very simple and inexpensive. As money started coming in, I upgraded some of the furniture, but the bed and tables are the same I started with. (See Chapter 3 for what you should start with). Once I got my basic room set up, I placed an ad on Craigslist and was open for business. That was before I even made a website! That work can come later. Within one week, I booked my first guest!

My point here is you can fast track the entire operation, as long as the space you create is **nice**. If you can quickly put a space together that *you* would feel comfortable sleeping and spending time in…just do it. If not, go to work to create that space. The trick to creating an attractive space is to not go overboard with stuff or details. Keeping your set up *simple* is usually better.

Please don't worry about not having a separate unit, remember that countless homeowners earn very good money running boarding house style rentals, (renting space in their main residence) without having a separate stand-alone building. My husband currently commutes four days a week to Southern California from our home in Northern California. We have him quite comfortably set up renting a room in a home for a price much cheaper than any hotel or his own apartment. It's a beautiful home and the owners renting to him are thrilled to have him— and his money. And he's just as thrilled for a safe, convenient place as his home away from home. Everyone wins.

Decades ago, rooming and boarding houses were common and often a preferred form of short-term housing. The "boarding house" is a popular and beloved setting in countless works of literary fiction and film. Although boarding houses have declined in popularity on the silver screen, in real life all around the world, they abound. I stayed in a woman's home in Austria on a trip to Europe years ago. She lived alone in a grand nine-bedroom chalet in a small village, and would rent rooms to people traveling around Europe. I will never forget her or her hospitality. We paid her less than a hotel would have cost, and she provided us the adventure of her small village in the Alps.

People running boarding house type rentals have the benefit of offering additional amenities, such as home cooked meals, personal assistant, or chauffeur services to their guests. Not only can you customize services, you can certainly boost your rates accordingly. Many foreigners enjoy living under the same roof with a real American family, experiencing a different culture firsthand. And of course, you could always simply offer a room without any additional hospitality. Tons of these are advertized on airbnb.com.

If you have an existing guesthouse, a garage you can convert, or even an extra room in your house— you can begin immediately to create, manage, and market a successful vacation rental that just about runs itself!

If you choose to convert a garage for instance, it needs to be clean, well insulated, with heat, possibly air conditioning— and a bathroom. It needs to be *livable.* I have seen a few really nice converted garages that are excellent vacation rentals. The great thing about converted garages is you can usually have a separate entrance. This type of situation may take a little longer if you have to implement any construction and plumbing.

If you happen to own a "destination" vacation rental, great.... this guide can help boost your traffic and fine-tune your operation. Those owning such rentals usually rely on outside property management companies who service multiple properties, maintaining accounting, marketing and most important maintenance. This type of management is necessary for remote rentals because it's pretty hard to piece together vendors you can feel good about that you don't even know! Imagine getting a call at 3:00 AM (from a different time zone) finding that something such as the pipes froze in your condo, and the family who traveled far to stay in *your* vacation rental high in the mountains had no water! Management companies offer a great service for such scenarios, but usually for a hefty price.

I have managed to assemble a team of trusted important maintenance people I count on when needed, saving myself a monthly management fee. They are my plumber, handyman, and Internet expert (as I provide Internet access in my rental). They are all only a phone call away and have worked with us for years.

So start now. Start simple and manage your rental by yourself—
you can pay someone later when you are making a stream of
money…if you choose to.

# CHAPTER 3

## Set up your space

---

*"Here is a simple but powerful rule - always give people more than what they expect to get."* - NELSON BOSWELL

---

Here is where the fun starts! I personally loved setting our room up! When you take the time to make this comfortable from the start, you won't have much to change as time goes on.

Just short of a tent in someone's backyard, I have seen every possible set up advertised as a vacation rental that you can imagine. The ones that I have seen most frequently are:

a) guesthouse

b) granny unit

c) converted garage

d) room/suite/wing in a main house

e) standard sublet (where tenant vacates their main resident short term)

f) pool houses

g) trailers / rv's (yes, people rent these and some are quite nice as long as they have a bathroom)

h) yurts (not so much in the city unless the property is large enough)

i) small pre-fab (kit) houses such as those featured on tumbleweedtinyhouses.com

j) house boats

I actually once saw a vacation rental on Craigslist for a *camper* attached to a truck! I guess if it's comfortable and the price is right, anything goes. I don't think that would work so well without a bathroom.

Which category do you fit into?

## THE BASICS OF YOUR SETUP

You will want to make this as easy on your guests as possible while not being cost prohibitive on your part. You certainly want to be *almost* as accommodating as a hotel, minus 24-hour service of any kind.

Don't make the mistake of offering too much, because then people will have more expectations of you. You are not a hotel, and you are not charging hotel prices. It's a good idea to give people that impression from the start, so be sure to list on your website all the details of exactly what you do and don't provide. This will save all those emails or calls asking if you provide a hair dryer, extra fold out bed, or whatever.

Okay, first things first...whatever space you have decided to use you will want to keep everything very simple. My motto is; *comfortable, attractive and basic.* Please consider that people have different styles and taste, and less is usually more. You may need to be able to visualize a *new* space, one not cluttered with your things. A space with just the basics for a short term stay.

I started with a totally empty space. Our room was already painted with calming, warm earth tones, so we didn't have to paint. But if you are starting with white walls, that's fine, just be prepared to touch them up to keep them fresh looking. If your walls are a bold color like red, that's fine too, as long as your décor is simple and your furniture matches and is minimal.

### DECOR: Don't go overboard!

You really want to avoid any kind of clutter of "stuff" you might be tempted to display, and there will be less dust that you or your cleaning person have to clean if you eliminate the tchotchke's and bric-a-brac!

By keeping the décor very simple, you won't need a theme and people won't get bored by a theme they wish could be changed up. For example, by a theme I mean it's probably not best to make your place look like the ultimate beach shack (unless of course you *are* located at the beach).

Your aunt might make the cutest needlepoint prairie houses that once framed will make her glow with pride, but think about what every high end hotel offers. They offer simple, classic style. That simplicity often equates cleanliness to many people, which is surely what you are going for. You can go modern contemporary, high tech, country comfortable, ranch, whatever style fits your architecture, but keep it simple because simple is classy.

Our walls feature one simple original abstract painting which adds some color and saved us money, large white wooden letters that spell out **C R E A T E** that we display on a single mounted wall shelf, a whimsical vintage metal poster on the same kind of shelf, a small decorative mirror with hooks that guests can hang a light bag or purse on, and two very small café style signs in the kitchenette. Our bathroom also has a very simple wall mirror (in addition to the above the sink cabinet mirror), and only two small landscape wall plaques.

If design is not your thing, ask someone who's style you admire for their opinion. Go find a design magazine that features *simple* room plans. I tried to create a space as if it were for a treasured friend who was coming to visit that I wanted to make feel special and pampered.

Ask yourself what would make you feel like releasing a sigh of relief and surprise if you were traveling, probably a bit weary and were walking into an unknown place for the first time. What would make you feel like you found a home away from home?

Once again, I don't mean to insult anyone here because you may have style that exceeds Martha Stewart's, but let's just say you don't. If you do have a sense of style and décor, please just skip ahead in your reading here. But for the sake of those (like me) who may be starting with a jumble of mismatched furniture, or might be storing your grandmothers antique hutch in your collection of hand me down pieces of furniture from one of your previous phases of life, please consider carefully what you need and don't need regarding "stuff".

## THE BED: Make it comfy!

You will need a *GREAT BED*! Obviously the bed is the focal point of any guest/hotel room, so make sure the bed location is the perfect place to "feature" the bed. There is no need to spend a lot of money on the head and foot boards ... (we personally furnished our entire room with everything from Ikea except the mattress and kept our set up costs way down). The bedframe we got is raised up a bit and the bed came with two drawers that roll out from under the bed. This is great because it's a place to store extra blankets. Our room is just one room with one closet, so we really need to maximize our storage.

Depending on the size of your space, you can go with a king bed if you like, but a queen size bed is perfect for two people, (we have a maximum occupancy of only two people). A queen bed also makes your room appear more spacious and unless you have a huge or separate bedroom where the bed will be, the aesthetic appeal of space is invaluable.

Once you select the bed location, sit or lay down on it and then simply figure out the placement of everything else you will need in the room. This is obvious and I don't mean to suggest that you won't know how to set up a room, but you would be surprised at the set up of some rentals that some people advertise! Some set ups make absolutely no sense at all. Even though our set up is perfect for most people, I have had people actually rearrange the furniture in my place!

The best tip regarding the bed is to *spend some money on a great mattress*! You don't have to have top of the line, we started with just an "okay" mattress and after we had a chunk of money sitting around from the flow of people who found us, we upgraded and then people started to notice how GREAT the bed was!

I keep my eyes open for sales on comfortable sheets (sometimes high end sometimes not), blankets, and duvet (washable only) covers, and our linens gradually went from just basic fare to higher quality. It is worth spending some money on this. If you want to spend the money for high thread count Egyptian cotton go ahead, that's a great feature to advertise on your web site. There is no bigger turn off than dingy, scratchy or old looking sheets. Bed Bath & Beyond, Anna's Linens and Costco are all great sources for linens.


**FURNITURE**: Simple & functional

Remember; *comfortable, attractive and basic*, are the only adjectives you need here. Again, you don't need high end. You only need the basics and it's always best to go minimal so you don't have the feeling of clutter. I know this too sounds a bit over simplified, but please don't make the mistake of imposing your idea of "charm". We stayed in a vacation rental along the coast of Sonoma last year and all of the furniture was mismatched and very old. Instead of feeling charming and cozy, it felt like an afterthought. Most people respond to simple, clean luxury. However sentimental you are about furniture you may have, remember the objective is just to make your guests comfortable. Any history you have with things, your guests will not even appreciate.

You will need matching bed side tables with simple, easy to use lamps. We have pharmacy style lamps so our guests can adjust the light themselves with some flexibility. We use energy efficient light bulbs only. Our bedside tables also have a small shelf where guests can place their personal items as well as small cabinets under the shelves where we store a variety of books. One of our bedside tables has a simple, clock radio so our guests may have an alarm clock handy. It's also a great place for small note pads and pens.

A media cabinet is essential if you provide a TV, and can also function as a place for extra storage if needed. We have a double sided medium cabinet with glass doors placed against a wall just opposite the bed. The television sits on top of it, along with a satellite box as we provide satellite TV. The inside has shelves where we keep the DVD player, and we also provide the added perk of a collection of DVD's that we buy from yard sales. People have commented time and again what a bonus this is, especially because they are not charged to watch the movies. One woman came from Texas to Los Angeles for some plastic surgery and was thrilled that she could hide out in our bungalow while she recovered and watch our complimentary movies all day! The cabinet also has a heavy duty flashlight for emergencies.

Now, you do not *have* to offer a TV, but most people will want that.We stayed in a place earlier this year along the Mendocino coast that had no TV or Internet! It was actually quite nice once we got over the initial shock of being completely unplugged.

If you are renting a room in your house—a TV is not expected. Just make sure you make that clear on your website or your Craigslist ad. Many TV's can be enjoyed with head phones so that noise isn't a factor if you are renting a room in your house. The room my husband rents while he works out of town does not have a TV. He often watches movies on his lap top computer with his headphones. That's very quiet for everyone.

Unless you have the space for a full sized sofa, a love seat or chaise lounge is a nice touch for a comfortable place to sit without having to be on the bed. It's bigger than a overstuffed chair, and just enough room for two people or one person to lay out comfortably. You really don't need a full size couch and in fact I don't recommend it. Some people might see it invitation to bring more people than agreed on to sleep in the room.

Our love seat is a chocolate brown leather one from Ikea, and you honestly cannot tell the difference between it and one that you buy at a high end store. We place a few soft pillows and a chenille throw blanket on the love seat, and people have commented on how cozy it is to just relax or read on.

We also have a floor lamp next to the love seat that matches the bed side tables. In front of the love seat, we have a small simple wooden chest that serves as a coffee table and opens to store extra

42

blankets. It is not too big, but compliments the style and size of the love seat and the extra storage is a real plus!

One side of the room has a nice work/dining table with two chairs. An adequate table can function as a place to eat, to arrange some magazines, a guest book for all of the great feedback you will be getting, along with a binder notebook that provides the details of your guest services.

The very important **Guest Services Book** is a binder style notebook that includes the following information:

1) My contact info

2) Wi-fi passcodes

3) Details of cleaning - we provide light cleaning for reservations of 7 or more days. We also explain here that there is no linen service.

4) TV/DVD instructions including which remote is for which device

5) Heating/AC instructions

6) Check out time

7) Local dining/shopping suggestions with menus

8) Instructions for taking trash out, if needed

With a detailed Guest Services Book, people won't have to call you at all hours with any of the above questions. This book is a huge component of making this operation *automatic*, so don't the mistake of excluding this book.

Another book on the table is a different type of guest book. It's an all occasion decorative Guest Book that you can pick up in a stationary store, or order online. This is the kind of book that you usually see at weddings where guests sign in. These books are usually bound and lined. We print a large custom sticky label with the name of our rental, and and invite people to let us know something about themselves such as the date of their visit, where they are from and the reason they came to town. Most of them are eager to sign the book and 99.9% of those that write in this book use the space to compliment our rental!

I read all of these entries and transfer them as reviews on my website and any vacation rental website that I advertise on. These comments really help to sell new bookings! In fact, you will find out just how comfortable you are making people feel by reading the comments in your guest book. If you aren't getting comments and thank you's for a positive and special experience that they will never forget, you will need to tweak your operation…and fast.

Our table is stained to match the armoire and coffee table and has two very nice chairs that compliment it. The table has a vase with very real looking silk flowers, as many people have allergies to fresh flowers. I know from experience. When I first opened my rental business, I would buy fresh flowers, **and** fill a small basket with fruit, chocolate and crackers! But since I am not running a

Bed & Breakfast or a hotel, none of that is necessary and its certainly too much work and expense for you! I do occasionally stock some individually wrapped chocolates in a nice bowl on either the table or the coffee table, but not always. It's a nice touch, and very inexpensive, so it's up to you.

Unless you have a very large room, or a room with a separate living area, this is all the furniture you need. Once again, simple is better and easier for you to maintain and replace when needed.

**STORAGE**: You'll need to have some

If your room does not have a closet, you will want to consider a standing armoire where people can hang a few items of clothing. We have a small walk-in closet where we have a sizable armoire to lock up linens and supplies.

On the subject of linens, we don't provide daily linen service, and most vacation rentals don't. Unless you want to tackle laundry every day, you probably won't want to offer this luxury. We do keep a couple of extra towels on hand on a shelf in the closet. You really don't want people using three towels a day per person like they might in a hotel, so it's best if you are going to store linens in the room, to have a locked cabinet somewhere.

Before I limited the linen supplies to my guests, my laundry piles were double what they are now after moving the linens extra to a locked cabinet. Double laundry equals double time and money for you or whomever you pay to do your laundry. Although they are a nice touch, we don't provide robes. High end hotels have them, but you pay with high end hotel rates. You can offer them, but be prepared for extra laundry, and of course they could disappear.

Our storage closet also has an ironing board, iron with the operating manual sitting on some mounted shelves, a small step ladder, extra pillows with clean pillow cases and a nice dowel for guests to hang some clothes using the wooden hangers provided, avoid wire hangers because they look cheap and don't hold up well. We also keep on hand a lint tape roller which sits on top of a low standing cubby hole type cabinet where guest can keep shoes, and folded clothes.

**KITCHEN/KITCHENETTE:** If you have one.

If your space does not have a kitchen or kitchenette, I would recommend that you keep only 2 small bottles of water as a courtesy on the table and not go to the trouble of providing any kind of makeshift "cooking" area.

I really believe this will avoid opening a big can of worms for you. If you don't have a kitchen that is up to code for cooking, don't even go there trying to provide something half baked for improvising. If you insist on something, limit it only to a microwave on a <u>very solid</u> surface or shelf. The last thing anyone wants is an accident and you sure don't need the liability!

I like to check out the competition usually when I travel and always try to stay in other vacation rentals. I have stayed in places that provide kitchens with the ability to cook a 6 course meal and in some places you can't even make a cup of coffee.

46

If a kitchen is offered, pretty much 100 % of the time, it is up to the guests of a vacation rental to clean the kitchen and leave it the way they found it. Most people do respect that, and I only provide very limited cooking options, but still some people occasionally leave a mess despite a rental agreement that says they need to leave the kitchenette as they found it.

Decide on your rules and include them in your rental agreement! I charge an extra cleaning fee of $25 minimum to those who leave a mess. It's best that people know this up front, so if you do have to charge, you can remind them it is stated in the rental agreement that they signed.

If you have a kitchen/kitchette, I recommend just these basics:

1)    A small size refrigerator (unless you have the space for a full sized one).

2)    Microwave oven

3)    Coffee maker -I use a single *one* cup brewer! After replacing 2 broken glass pots in the past, I was happy to find the single-cup, pod brewer that I bought online, (coffeewholesaleusa.com). The coffee pods are so easy you just put the serving cup under the brew spout, load the pod, water and voila..a freshly brewed single cup of coffee. Clean up of a pot is eliminated and the size is small for storage. The premium coffees are relatively inexpensive.

4) Sugar and dry or liquid creamer (individually packaged for sanitation and convenience).

5) Toaster.

6) Electric tea pot (safer than micro-waving a cup of water and we get many Europeans who must have their tea).

That is all we provide. People have no problem making their coffee with tap water and if they want something different, they can usually go to the market and bring back a big jug of filtered water, which when left behind I use to water my outdoor plants and fill the ice tray. Of course if you have the space, an electric hot plate makes it possible for people to heat some pasta, soup, or a simple dish. They will appreciate this, but you need to consider the additional power expense and clean up. I keep my price point pretty low and most people are expecting to eat out mostly, or just have snack items, salads, etc. in my bungalow.

Many people contact me wanting to be able to really cut their costs by cooking their own meals, and I understand that. I also choose to have very minimal cooking availability because I DON'T want any of the following worries or considerations:

1) The fire risk.

2) Extra time cleaning up pot and pans and dishes.

3) Lingering smells of foods that might be offensive to someone checking in after someone has cooked.

4) The extra expense of stocking and maintaining kitchen necessities.

5) Injuries from hot oil or other burns.

Our kitchenette has some counter space and cupboards where we keep drinking glasses, coffee cups, a small cutting board with one sharp knife, one pyrex measuring cup, a microwave safe bowl, eating utensils and dishes for **two** people only, which makes clean up when guests leave much easier than if you have plates for eight people. Most people who stay in our guest house treat it as their own home, but on occasion you will get guests who don't wash their dishes during their stay, and the fewer dishes you provide, the fewer you or your cleaning person will have to clean up. As a rule of thumb, you should supply no more dishes than twice the maximum occupancy.

You will want to avoid left over food of any kind. (Even with the minimal cooking allowed in my bungalow, people still leave leftover food). Personally, I throw it all out. I know this can seem a bit wasteful, but I don't think it's a good idea to leave any food left for the next guests.

I am not willing to risk any liability from food left behind. It's best to avoid any clutter in an already compact kitchenette. Clutter to me always translates to a question of cleanliness, and I don't think anyone wants to spend time wondering about that.

Under our small kitchen sink we stock paper towels, basic cleaner, and a linen kitchen towel which gets changed out when the room gets turned around for each new reservation.

The sink should always have a clean sponge, dish washing and hand soap, and unless your kitchen has an automatic dishwasher, you can get a small dish rack for draining dishes on the counter top.

## THE BATHROOM: Make yours special!

The bathroom is one of the first places people want to see pictures of when they ask about my rental. You want to pay attention and make it squeaky clean, and *inviting.* The two most effective ways of creating a wow factor here is with lighting and paint! Put dimmer switches on your overhead lights, use soft lighting to accent whatever color you have chosen for the bathroom. Just Google "lighting tips for bathrooms" and you can spend hours finding something you like. The great thing is lighting and paint are both relatively inexpensive but makes a real statement. You should avoid overhead fluorescent lighting at all costs! Nobody looks good under a fluorescent light, that is for sure.

Our bathroom has a beautiful large shower with glass doors and no bathtub. Because of the glass we have to keep it looking new, removing water deposits and taking special care each week to make sure it's cleaned properly. The shower/bath should *always* be immaculate and sanitized in between guests. Our shower stays stocked with large pump plastic bottles of shampoo, conditioner and body wash. All are easy to refill and you don't have the waste or run the risk of spreading bacteria that you would with

50

individual soap bars. You certainly would never leave a used bar of soap for new guests. Costco is a great source for these supplies, and I use a brand of body wash that I can find in the local drugstore. You'll want to make sure that your hair and body products aren't too heavily scented.

We keep fresh oversize thick luxurious towels from Costco (another good investment so you don't have to constantly replace cheaper ones) hanging on the outside of the shower door rack, and on the inside rack we keep a bath mat. One note about towels: I used to buy white but over time, white just doesn't hold up as well as ivory or a similar off white color. I would advise against any bright or dark color, as the constant washings these towels require will fade colored towels very quickly.

We also have a decorative robe hook on the bathroom wall for guests to hang any robe or nightclothes that they would bring themselves. There is a rug with non-slip backing on the bathroom floor that is large enough to cover most of the entire bathroom width, because nobody needs an opportunity for a guest to slip on a wet floor. Always consider your liability.

The bathroom should have plenty of toilet paper (individually wrapped which you can buy at Costco) ready to be used with extra rolls available. Our bathroom sink has a cupboard underneath where we keep the extra paper and a hair dryer. We used to keep a small area heater for cold mornings, but we took it away—because again, I always worried about the liability. There is heat in the room so people can just heat the room up if needed.

## COURTYARD /PATIO /GARDEN: A special treat!

Although your guests will most likely spend their waking hours out doing what they came to town to do, many people on vacation want to sit outside if the weather permits. I have a small courtyard just for them, that is off limits to anyone else. If you can provide such a space, it's a plus!

The courtyard features a small table with umbrella, chairs, potted plants and we plan to install a wall fountain soon. My place is located in Southern California and many people can't wait to soak up the sun when visiting. They love the courtyard for enjoying morning coffee or a glass of wine in the afternoon. We've added some inviting solar plant lights that come on each night. It's a nice touch that is inexpensive and requires no additonal electricity or maintenance.

As mentioned earlier, our main residence has a hot tub and in the early days of running my rental, we let people use it during certain hours. When I found out that my insurance would not cover any claim with a short term rental, I no longer provided access to the hot tub, and it has not impacted interest in my rental at all. These are issues to be very clear on with your insurance company, as well as your guests.

## PRIVACY: It's super important for everybody

When we first started renting our bungalow, although it was a stand alone detached unit several feet away from our main house, both structures looked out onto my backyard living area. We have a two level yard. The top level is our main house and a nice yard.

The lower level has a detached garage and across from that is the guest bungalow along with the courtyard. Although the bungalow has a private entrance from outside the gated property, once inside, guests used to have a clear and open view into my yard and my family room. I in turn, had a totally unobstructed view of them coming and going or hanging outside to smoke or talk on the phone or whatever.

This was fine for awhile, but I was really aware at how awkward this occasionally was as I saw people hurry in and out. I also felt like I was in a fish bowl at times just going into my own backyard with our son.

So we decided to create some kind of barrier for privacy. The two levels of our yard have a brick retaining wall, so we attached a row of wooden lattice panels to the wall and lined one side with potted plants for more privacy. That division was so effective that after we had some money saved from the rental income, we then invested in a full on custom fence which was perfect, providing total privacy from the main house and our vacationing guests.

Any detail regarding privacy is really something to strive for. Although not completely necessary, if you can set up a situation where people feel they have their own space, that is a real attraction to them. A private entrance is optimum and makes the guest feel most comfortable.

Remember, these are *ideal* situations and you don't need to start with a courtyard, fences etc. It took us two years to come to that. But once we did, it was much better for everyone. Even if you rent a room out in your house, you will want to consider the privacy issue.

I know a guy in Northern California who runs a Bed and Breakfast in his house. He remodeled this house just to run a B&B and it's a super popular place to stay. His place features a private stairway from inside his front entry door that leads up to three amazing rooms all with views. Each room features it's own small but beautifully appointed bathroom. He has his entire rental business all on the top floor!

His ground floor has two large bedrooms with bathrooms, a large entertainers kitchen, laundry room and open living room where he, his wife and young daughter live. He has one side of his outside large patio for guests, and a different private area for his daughter. He also cooks meals for his guests and becomes friends with many of them, who all usually return to his place. His entire operation is set up in a way that although everyone is under one roof, they all have privacy!

But please realize there are plenty of people who **successfully** rent rooms in their house who don't have the interest in a B&B set up. The woman named Elizabeth who was mentioned earlier, offers a detached unit, as well as a master suite in her main house. She can benefit from multiple guests at the same time—if she wants, but she doesn't *have to.* She sometimes has people staying in her detached unit for months at a time, and still rents out a room in her house, under the same roof she lives in.

She lives alone and feels comfortable with this arrangement as she provides different packages that include some cooking, laundry or running errands if desired. Her situation can be like a B&B, but it is located right in her house or her backyard depending on which package is chosen. If you are having guests in your home, you can provide these extras, and charge for them.

The main thing to consider here would certainly be your comfortability and safety and I would think some privacy. When she has people staying in her house, she sort of keeps herself limited to certain rooms while they are there and this works fine for all concerned. I know that she has a secure way of screening guests, as do I, and this is the main thing to focus on if people will be staying under your roof.

Let's just wrap up the topic of different kinds of set-ups mentioned in Chapter 3. Most of them are pretty self explanatory and you get the picture that you can either have a situation in your primary residence or a stand alone unit. Any and all situations can be made to be a four star experience, or grossly inadequate. That is all up to you.

But I want to mention garages in particular. As mentioned earlier, I have seen many of them converted into rentals, but the trick here is to make sure it doesn't *look* like a garage when you are ready to do business. I have been absolutely appalled at some pictures people have posted on Craigslist (especially in San Francisco) with "converted garages"!

Remember, guests should feel good about entering day or night, and any space you create should have *all* of the modern conveniences and necessities needed. Any converted garage should certainly be insulated and warm or have a great heater and air conditioning…..and a nice bathroom! It can be done, as many people convert their garages for extra family living spaces, home offices, gyms, art studio's, and play rooms. This is in fact one of the easier ways to start and very often a garage will have a separate entry door which is great for privacy, or it's pretty simple to cut a wall and install a door.


**SAFETY EQUIPMENT:** So everyone can relax!

Do keep safety in mind for the necessary décor, such as a non-slip rug next inside the doorway. Many of your guests will come in at night or during rain and, and even if your

place is completely carpeted, a non-slip rug is a good idea. Make sure all wall hangings and the TV (if you have one) are secured and cannot fall on someone.

It is imperative and REQUIRED by law and most insurance companies for any vacation rental to have a VISIBLE fire extinguisher!!

We actually have ours visibly displayed and bolted onto the wall in our kitchenette. It's a simple clamp bolt that you can easily and quickly pull the extinguisher from at any time.

I also suggest some emergency flashlights. We keep two emergency flashlights in the room plugged into electric wall plates to keep charged at all times. These types of flash lights turn on once they are taken out of the electric socket, or if the power fails. And of course don't forget a smoke alarm. We actually have two smoke alarms, one in the kitchenette and one near the entrance of the unit (another insurance requirement).

Another thing to consider is keeping a first aid kit on hand. This is a small price to pay that will give you and your guests peace of mind.

**KEYLESS IS THE WAY TO GO! :** The most convenient tool yet!

When we first started our rental, we used keys to enter the bungalow. This is the obvious choice for most people. Just about everyone uses keys to get into a door. I spent valuable time hunting down interesting little key chains that might bring a smile to someone or at least convince him or her that I had a sense of humor. Not necessary at all. Because, if I wasn't home to meet and greet them, *someone* had to hand them a key! I can assure you, I broke into a sweat numerous times over this baffling problem.

I actually found a place in the yard where I would hide a key, if I weren't home when someone arrived. What I awkwardly discovered was that giving directions for a hidden key to people who are arriving to a strange place, often in the dead of night, isn't easy--or very professional. The last thing they want is a treasure hunt to figure out how to navigate the way to their bed! And of course you would never want to get a call at 3:00 AM that the tenant has lost the key after a night on the town, and needs you to let them in.

I remembered friends who had a keyless combination pad on their front door because they seemed to constantly lose their keys. So, I went down to my local Home Depot and found combination keypad systems to mount on the entrance gate and the door to the bungalow. Using that system, I am able to change codes in between guests, and also issue regular guests their own personal codes. This makes everything simpler for everyone. There is no risk of someone losing or copying a key, and your guests will really appreciate such a well thought out detail.

The absolute best thing about the keyless system was more *freedom*! I no longer had to greet people the moment they arrived as I had from the beginning. I no longer had to schedule my time around the arrival times of the guests!

The entire point of this book is to impress upon you how **automatic** your rental can be. The minute I didn't have to *hand someone a key*, it gave everyone more freedom. I no longer had constant interruptions in my life. My guests, usually weary from their travels, wouldn't have to be "on" just to get in the door! And they could easily leave on their own schedule, without having to turn their key in!

Your place should be set up so that anyone can walk in—at any time—with **everything** they need right there in front of them; without **you** having to show them!

Okay, that's the basics of the room, remember…provide the basics, but don't go overboard with things that will cost you more money, time, or clutter your space.

# CHAPTER 4

## Cleanliness really is next to Godliness!

---

*"Style is an option, clean is not"* - TIDE DETERGENT

---

A lack of cleanliness is a deal breaker for most people! Whether you do the cleaning yourself or have a team working for you, ***all maintenance*** is crucial. The best possible way to cover yourself, or anyone else that will be cleaning for you is to create a time saving and detailed cleaning checklist (included here at the end of chapter). If you are not going to do the cleaning yourself, you must find the best employee to clean your place and keep them invested in your rental.

When we first started our rental, I did all of the cleaning/laundry and my husband did any maintenance needed. It was entirely easy for me because I was home all of the time and my son was in pre-school a few mornings a week. It's funny what pride can encourage in a person. I hated, really loathed cleaning my own house, but when I went out to the bungalow to get it ready for an arriving guest, I would get a bit excited and actually look forward to the whole process!

It felt great that I could create a space that always put a smile on someone's face when they walked in and saw our place. It's kind of like the feeling of having a new car as a teenager and spending a few hours washing and waxing it and then giving your friends a ride. Except for the part where you get paid to have guests stay at your place.

But, back to cleaning. I knew when I cleaned that place, it was close to perfect. I knew I could count on someone being in the shower with complete confidence that it had been scrubbed and sanitized. I knew if someone gave my shelves the white glove treatment, they would find no dust! I knew how comfy and fresh smelling the sheets would be when they crawled into bed. I knew if they put their shoes under the bed and reached down to retrieve them and sneaked a peak under where they slept, no dust bunnies would be found! Those are all very important things to me when staying in a hotel or anywhere for that matter.

When I got too busy to do the cleaning myself, I started hiring people I found from Craigslist. After training about *four* different people, one of who worked out pretty well for awhile, I realized that I needed to find someone I could absolutely rely on. Some of these people would schedule my time, say they needed the money and then not show up! Or they would show up late and and I would have to get started to have the place ready for arriving guests. There was always the stress of never knowing if they were going to do a good job.

Besides that, we were talking about moving away and I wasn't really sure I could keep my rental going if I wasn't on site. It was a difficult time because I didn't quite know how to solve this problem.

I then wondered if maybe I had a *friend*, someone I could count on and trust and who was flexible who might want a small part time job. Well, the perfect person popped into my head and the real bonus was that she lives only one block away!

Irene has been expertly cleaning my place for about 4 ½ years now. I call on her (and I pay her nicely) to clean and do many things in my absence. She also decided that I was spending too much money on a professional laundry service for the linens (lucky me), and I now pay her less than I used to pay them, and it helps her out too! She takes the same kind of pride in keeping the place as clean as I did.

Now this obviously costs me more money than when I was cleaning the place myself. But, I took a chance and raised my rates, not knowing if this would diminish my business or not, and it turns out that I actually attracted a better *clientele* overall. So my increase in rates, takes care of my payments to her and I still end up making great profits.

Hiring a friend was the best thing I ever did. The only problem was she is only one person, and if she has a conflict, or gets sick, than what? Well I went back to that list of friends and asked someone else to be a back up person for cleaning and she said yes. Problem solved. If you can't clean your rental yourself, ask a friend and have another friend as the back up. This is the best advice I can offer for your security in this area if you are not doing your own cleaning.

I am lucky enough to have found the people I can rely on and I make sure they feel appreciated. Whenever I am in town where my rental is, I take Irene out to a nice meal. A Christmas time, I give the people who help run my business MONEY. Everyone needs and likes money at Christmas. I value them so much, I pay them well for their minimal time spent and they have an investment in me and my place. I also offer them full use of my rental whenever they want, provided there is a vacancy. They are both people who take pride in what they do. That is what you need if you cannot clean your rental yourself.

Using the following detailed cleaning checklist, *anyone* can walk into your place and get it in top shape for your guests. You can use my checklist as your template, and alter it as needed. Make your work as automatic as you can if you use others to help you. You can't afford to miss anything when it comes to cleanliness!

**GUEST HOUSE CLEANING CHECK LIST:**

All linens (sheets and towels) are located in pine cabinet in the walk in closet. The combination to open is -----. **PLEASE LOCK IT AGAIN AFTER YOU FINISH.**

**BED:**

\_\_\_\_ change sheets and pillowcases and duvet cover.

\_\_\_\_ dust the wood on the bed with furniture polish.

**KITCHEN:**

\_\_\_\_ wash and put away dishes.

_____ clean kitchen counter.

_____ clean inside microwave.

_____ clean inside of refrigerator / wipe down outside of refrigerator.

_____ clean coffee pot.

_____ sweep floor and wipe down with damp rag and a bit of floor cleaner.

_____ empty trash and put fresh trash bag in waste basket.

_____ leave new dishtowel hanging on door under sink.

**FURNITURE** - (use a small soft cloth and spray furniture polish)

_____ dust tables.

_____ dust wood shelves on walls.

_____ dust bedside tables (inside and outside).

_____ wipe down bedside lamps (use soft damp cloth, but DO NOT use furniture polish).

_____ clean baseboards of room when needed.

**WINDOWS**

_____ spray inside windows with Windex and if needed outside too.

_____ wipe down inside of window ledges with a damp cloth and a bit of cleaner.

## VACUUM

_____ vacuum the entire room.

_____ vacuum under bed.

_____ vacuum entryway floor.

## BATHROOM

_____ spray shower with non-scrub cleaner, rinse and then dry the shower off.

_____ clean glass doors on both sides with Windex.

_____ clean toilet with bowl cleaner and scrub with bowl brush.

_____ wipe down the toilet seat, seat cover and the toilet base with all-purpose cleaner.

_____ spray the entire toilet and shower with Lysol, please leave the Lysol under sink.

_____ clean bathroom sink with non-scrub cleaner.

_____ clean mirrors with Windex (above sink and on wall).

_____ shake out bathroom rug outside in dirt on side of building.

_____ sweep bathroom floor and wipe down with small amount of floor cleaner.

_____ empty trash and put fresh trash bag in wastebasket.

_____ put new towels in bathroom (2 bath, 2 hand, 2 washcloths).

_____ leave 2 extra bath towels on shelf in walk in closet.

**RUGS**

_____shake out entryway rug and bathroom rug outside.

_____sweep exterior entry way outside door.

**DRY EVERYTHING DOWN AFTER IT IS CLEANED SO NOTHING LOOKS WET AND <u>CALL</u> ME WITH ANY QUESTIONS. THANKS SO MUCH!!!!!**

# CHAPTER 5

## Top-Notch Advertising and Marketing

---

*"If you make customers unhappy in the physical world, they might each tell 6 friends. If you make customers unhappy on the internet, they can each tell 6,000 friends"* - JEFF BEZOS

---

### THE INTERNET PRETTY MUCH RULES THE WORLD!

Unless you want to make flyers to hand out at the airport (I am kidding), all potential guests will be either from one of the many online sources you need to be using, or referrals. Embrace the Internet and *score* with a winning formula for success!

You may be an old pro at this, or you may be a beginner. Either way, the material covered here is really important to implement for maximizing your bookings.

Deciding where to spend your money and how to invest your time to advertise your vacation rental will be the difference between success and failure.

Once your place is set up, the quickest and easiest way to watching the money roll in is by taking advantage of the mega vacation rental site **airbnb.com**. This site is the best model for getting you going right away, without an upfront fee. You simply set up your account, create your profile, upload pictures and bingo, you are in business. They do have fees, but they only get paid when you get paid. They collect 3% of the total reservation amount that is booked from you, and then they collect a 6% or 12% guest fee that your guests pay them for.

Most of the other popular vacation rental third party sites, such as homeaway.com, charge an annual membership fee.

If you don't want to pay any fees and just to put your place out there, you can certainly do that, however you will gain more exposure by creating your own website, ad, *and* listing with airbnb.com.

I do very well using both airbnb.com and homeaway.com, but before I found them, I created my own **ad** and **website**. It's good to consider that as this industry grows and changes, you may want to secure parallel bookings from your own site as well as vacation rental third party sites. This will protect you against mergers, takeovers and changes in policies that come with using third party sites. Just a few years ago, VRBO was the biggest player in this industry and then homeaway.com came and bought them out.

Guests are able to find my site, which has gained momentum over time, from being out in cyberspace all these years. Often I have referrals who point people to my site, rather than find my rental on a third party website.

Don't let the idea of building your own website scare you too much. Very often you can find a student to do this for you, or there are several websites that can walk you through designing your own, for a reasonable price or free. I use Word Press (see resources)

Of course if you are not Internet savvy, you can always try old school advertising, but it is expensive, doesn't exactly directly target your market, and doesn't reach very many people. If you want to go this route anyway, I suggest you research places in your town that will allow you to put up flyers on bulletin boards, or publications to place free print ads. Such places could be, colleges, travel clubs, church *any* place you can think of that are points of interest to someone visiting your town. Colleges are good because so many relatives come to visit students living in dorms, and those people need places to sleep.

## YOUR EYE CATCHING AD

You can easily write a brief ad to put on Craigslist to get you started right away. The great thing about Craigslist is that it's *free and immediate*. There isn't anything (at least anything legal) that one can't find on Craigslist! And you don't have to be an Internet geek to put your ad up. To prove the power of Craigslist, the popular airbnb.com vacation rental site has a built in feature to add Craigslist as a source to advertise your rental when you place your listing with them. They know you will get many hits from Craigslist and they want a percentage of that.

My Craigslist ad includes current *pictures* of my main room, bathroom, courtyard, and kitchenette. People really want to see pictures of where they are going to live short term. I started with just photos we took ourselves. Then when we had some money we hired a professional photographer and it was one of the best investments that we ever made. He was able to use a much better camera and knew how to maximize the lighting to make the photos look more inviting that we ever could. It's easy enough to find someone affordable from Craigslist or Elance, which is another great resource to seek out.

The absolute best way to start is by spending some time viewing current vacation rental listings on Craigslist, in your city. What pops out at you when you read these? Unless you are in a really small town (which could be a big advantage to you due to lack of competition) you need to think about what you have to offer and find a way to *sell* that.

**HOW MUCH IS ENOUGH WITHOUT BEING GREEDY?**

Let's go over your price structure now, since most people will be searching price when they are skimming ads.

The good news is you are in charge here. And even better, chances are there are people right in your town who are your competitors. That's really great because you can go on Craigslist, Home Away, airbnb.com, or any other vacation rental site out there and actually see what rate is acceptable for the kind of set up you have. You can use what they have already tested in your own region as your guide.

When I started my rental, I didn't know about homeaway.com, and airbnb.com hadn't been born yet. How I decided my rate was by checking the rates of the hotels/motels located near my property. I figured if people were looking for somewhere to stay in my area, they would probably take a look at these hotels too. I started charging about 50% less per night than the hotels, plus I did not add any "occupancy tax", which is customary at hotels. The cheapest price was around $140.00 per night plus hotel tax which varies somewhere around between 8 and 12 percent in my state. Hotels often have parking fees and obviously the nicer the hotel, the higher the price. My rate compared to this was amazing and of course people would be interested in staying in the same neighborhood for a much lower rate.

I also checked out my local competitors listed on Craigslist, although there were not as many then as there are now. My formula for charging half of what hotels were mentioned above was inline with what other's were doing so that was good.

When I first started, I charged $75 per night, with no additonal tax or cleaning fee. This was a *steal* and brought people in right away. Over the years, as I have improved the property (privacy fences, better furniture etc.) I have raised it to $95 per night. When the recession was really bad last year, I lowered it to $85 per night. This is for any reservation two or more nights. One night only is $125.00, and I offer a discount for seven nights of $570, that is one full night free in that seven night block of time. I am also open to negotiating longer bookings if asked.

I always make sure to note on my web site that the tax and cleaning fee is already included in the nightly rate. People really like this, as most vacation rental properties charge at least a separate cleaning fee.

You really must not try to compete with the hotels. You are not in the hotel business. You are in the "self serve hospitality business". The hotels in your area are only good for referring guests who ask for an alternative in your area if you are already booked and they need a place to stay. Once they see what you charge compared to the local hotel, they will really appreciate your place! I have had people not be able to get into my place and then contact me way in advance on a return trip, just so they don't need to pay for a hotel.

The trick here is to be completely honest with yourself. Take a look around and see what others are doing. Be fair. Even the most thrifty person shopping for the best deal wants to feel like they are getting something special and that they are important. You must create an *experience* that will make a guest feel so lucky to have found you that they will keep coming back and will talk about your rental to everyone they know. You can create this experience by creating a wow factor with your set up.

It's best to charge by the night because you will get people who will say that they are checking in late, and leaving early and not even staying a full 24 hours, and sometimes they will want you adjust your rate because of this. Well that may be true for them, and this is an area where you should operate like a hotel, because *you* still have to have the time and expense to turn the room around. Only charge per night.

Okay, so once you have your price decided, you can always change it up or down to test the different responses you may get.

This is my current ad:

---

## $95 / 1br - 400ft² - L.A. - Charming private bungalow guesthouse rental - prime location! (Studio City - Sherman Oaks - L.A.) (map)

$95 per night /$125 One night only / $570/ week (tax and cleaning fee included.)
VISA/MASTERCARD/AMEX/DISCOVER

We are renting an ideal guesthouse vacation rental right in the middle of the best part of Los Angeles, just minutes from the major studios! We are right on the border of Studio City, North Hollywood, and Sherman Oaks in the cultural center of Los Angeles.

We get lots of repeat guests who are thrilled with the unit. It's the perfect vacation rental room for quick stopovers, business trips, or a romantic weekend or extended visit. The bungalow is like staying at a bed and breakfast without having to deal with the other people! It's really SUITE! Great Los Angeles lodging. There is free street parking.

Maximum occupancy: 2

Sorry - No pets.

Perfect L.A. accommodations. Better than a motel!

Learn more, read reviews and check availability here: http://www. link to your website/calendar or email if you don't have calendar

---

To sum up, think about why someone would come to your place. What is special about it. Do you have a prize winning garden where guests can enjoy their morning coffee? A view? Use of a pool or hot tub? Free and safe parking?

Some of the reasons guests come to my place is because of the location, the fact that it's a free standing privately gated unit with its own entrance, a small garden patio, is a relatively new building, has a great shower in the bathroom, and once inside they are completely charmed by the comfortable environment they find.

But mostly they come because for all of that and more, it costs them under $100 per night! They can't touch a nice hotel in the area for that. They can go on the outskirts of town in some very undesirable neighborhoods and get a price like mine or even cheaper—but they sure don't want to do that. With my low overhead, that $100 really starts adding up for me.

Carefully consider what you are offering. Many people who have never stayed at a vacation rental will question any risk involved. I did before I ever stayed in one. So what would be their motivation to stay in your place, if it's not cheaper and hopefully nicer than a hotel or motel?

What can you create and convey in your ad that will attract them to your place? I assure you that if you live in any metropolitan city, there are many people who are advertising vacation rentals. Just have a look at Craigslist, Homeaway.com and airbnb.com to see the numbers! You can compare the ads and plainly see what doesn't work and avoid mistakes others are making. You need to be competitive in your pricing and all the features that you offer. Remember—pictures sell a rental.

I am thrilled when guests choose my bungalow for the price, only to discover what one guest has called "...a truly hidden jewel".

## YOUR LIVING WEBSITE

I say *living* website, because if you don't keep adding to it, you will be buried in cyberspace quicker than a gopher running from a cat. You need to keep feeding those search engines to stay current in the almighty Google search engines and social networks.

Now on to your website. You certainly don't want to spend all of your time explaining your rental over and over again, either by phone or e- mail, so you'll need a great and ***effective*** web site to point people to. It's always a good idea to check your competition out online as well. Looking at your competitors' sites can give you great ideas of what is working for them, from design to the copy they have written in their ad.

You must include as many details as possible on your site. The traveler of today is very sophisticated and Internet savvy.

Remember, your potential guests may be *first time vacation rental customers*, so you need to sell them from your web site. Your job is to save your self and them a lot of time and frustration by clearly laying out what you are offering. Mystery usually unnerves people when shopping for anything on the Internet! In addition to selling the customer, the more content on a web site the better for search engines to find you.

Along with an inviting moniker and description of your rental, the number one priority on your site is **photos and more photos**! Yes, I know I am starting to sound like a broken record here, but go to any vacation rental website or Craigslist and see for yourself. You will spend more time looking at any listing with great photos.

You should have at least one great photo of the bed. Most people coming to your city vacation rental will be spending most of their time sleeping. It's doubtful they are coming to just hang out in the room.

Most of the questions I'm asked about our place is about the bed and the bathroom, so be sure to focus on those pictures. If you have any great feature to offer such as a courtyard or garden, make sure that is also on your site!  For instance if you offer any refreshments, you can set up an elegant still life photo of your coffee service, or maybe a bowl of fresh fruit, or whatever you are offering. You need to hook potential guests immediately, as many people will simply move on to one of your competitors if you don't catch them with some excellent photos.

In addition to photos, you will also need some detailed pertinent descriptions posted. This list should be as thorough as possible.

Our list is as follows:

---

## The California Bungalow

*A charming short-term vacation rental that beats the prices of hundreds of Los Angeles hotels, motels, bed & breakfasts, and other lodging.*

*400 Sq. ft. private bungalow suite

*Wireless connectivity

*Private entrance – semi - private courtyard

*Free-standing unit - no shared walls

*Satellite TV/DVD/CD

*Kitchenette

*Large Shower/bathroom

*Fully furnished

*Non-Smoking room

*Queen Bed with European pillow top mattress

*Free street parking

*Heating/Air conditioning

*Deposit required

*Visa/MasterCard/Discover/American Express

*Check in and check out times

*Maximum Occupancy

*Sorry - No Pets

*English and French spoken

---

Notice how listing everything with snappy bullet points instead of a hard to digest clunky paragraph is much easier to read.

In addition, we list our rates, or any special deals we are running. Without giving our exact address (for security reasons), we list our approximate location including the distance to several of the more popular landmarks located nearby.

It's important to state your maximum occupancy *very clearly* on your website so you don't waste anyone's time while they are skimming the details. I happen to have a single room of about 400 square feet and only one bed, which sleeps two people. I do not have room for more. You may have a much larger place, but should make your maximum occupancy policy very clear in your agreement.

If I am asked to make an exception of the number of guests allowed, I mention that I am not able to, due to insurance restrictions (which is true because of the size of the room). Besides that, I only have one bed and I do not allow any air- beds, sleeping bags (fire escape hazard) etc., to be brought in. On occasion, I make an exception if someone has *one* infant or small child as long as they are all willing to sleep in one Queen sized bed. You also limit the occupancy to avoid extra wear and tear and higher utility bills from more showers, electrical use, etc.

Our check in time is 3:00 PM and check out time is 11:00 AM and although you don't need to mention that in a Craigslist ad, you will want it on your website. You will also need to put these times on your rental agreement and confirmation letter that we will discuss in the next chapter. The window of time between check in and checkout is important to determine so you can allow enough cleaning time when someone leaves in the morning and someone else checks in the same day. It takes just about two hours to completely clean our place, yours may take more or less. You will need to decide on this and on top of that, give yourself a little bit of leeway.

Our rental agreement states we have a early check in / late check out fee, but honestly—I never enforce this. It's a better public relations move to just let people take advantage of this, *if the room is available.* These people are often traveling from far away, so if I can help them by getting them in early, I make an attempt to do so. Same as if they are leaving later in the day, but I can only do this *when* the schedule fits with my next reservation and my cleaning manager Irene.

As mentioned earlier, be sure to add all favorable guest comments left in your guest book or via email, to a section of your website where you can feature your reviews.

We also mention on our site that our bungalow is ultra-popular, and since we have just the one unit, the place books up quickly. If you are just starting out and cannot say this **truthfully**, consider posting something equally inviting on your web site like the following:

*"Whether you are coming to visit family, conduct business or just want to take in the sights, we offer an affordable, comfortable and unique alternative to a hotel, while visiting (name of your town)".*

Be sure to include any well-known points of interest in your town on your site. In fact, I suggest making a full web page on your site for each point of interest in your area. That way, if someone is searching for, let's say, The Golden Gate Bridge, Google may just take him or her to that page on your site. Be sure to post all the details of each point of interest such as a brief description, directions, hours of operation, and range of rates. Our website includes several pictures of popular and famous landmarks of our city, which can be found and downloaded from the Internet. Many people will search the web for accommodations *near* popular landmarks, so if your rental is located near any noteworthy attraction, it's *imperative* that you list that on your site. We make sure to include the distance to all such landmarks from our rental.

For instance, our bungalow is located in the heart of the entertainment capital of the world, and it's crucial we mention that and have a web page for that. Whether a guest is coming for business or wants to attend a taping of The Tonight Show, they at least know they are staying in the perfect neighborhood.

We also list local recommended restaurants, grocery stores, shopping centers, dry cleaners, and urgent-care center etc; located within walking distance of our unit. Most people travel with a computer or smart phone and can find many desired forms of entertainment, but guests coming from abroad may not be as plugged in because of foreign cell phone plans, etc, so it's best to include some community resources in the room itself, as well as on your site. Your guests will be very grateful and you will also be supporting your local merchants.

We send our guests to a great and really popular restaurant just one block from our bungalow—the owners are neighbors and friends. It's amazing knowing that many of our guests from all over the world have discovered the same excellent food that we have enjoyed for years, just a short walk away. And in turn, we help our neighborhood thrive. We keep the menu from this restaurant and a few others in our guest services book and that is much appreciated by our guests.

List any other language you may speak on your site! My husband speaks French, and has been able to help several times with our guests from France. We display the French flag on our site, as well as mention that both English and French are spoken by us. Remember that the search engines will look for all this info and find your site! Also, if you want to go the extra mile, try to have duplicate main pages in several languages for deeper search penetration.

For people who may not be visiting with a car, it's very helpful to include links for public transportation and airport shuttle service on your site. It's also helpful to provide the telephone number to a local taxi service.

We include a list of all amenities offered in our bungalow--from coffee or tea to the Egyptian cotton sheets (and don't forget to show the photo)! List as many details as possible on your web site because you save your time answering endless questions, and your guests save their valuable time asking!

**LIST YOUR STEPS FOR MAKING A RESERVATION!**

As you well know, many people are in a hurry all of the time. You don't want them moving on to another rental because they couldn't *quickly* figure out how to reserve the fabulous place you are offering! I have worked out just 3 short steps for securing a reservation, which are displayed ***clearly*** on my website. I can't emphasize enough how important it is to make this *easy* for people.

The 3 steps are:

- Step 1: **Check the availability** of your requested dates on our online calendar. (Provide link to calendar)

- Step 2: **If your dates are available, notify us** that you would like to reserve. We will send you the deposit info and rental agreement.

- Step 3: **Call or email us** with your credit card info for the deposit. At this time we block our online calendar with your dates, and send you a

84

confirmation along with all of the details for arriving. We do not save any dates without a deposit.

You will notice in Step 1 (checking availability), that the guest has been directed to view an accurate calendar.[3] They can plainly see if their desired dates are open or not.

Before I used this online feature, people would call or email me at all hours just to check availability! This step avoids me having to pick the phone up late at night to speak with a potential guest, as most people are coming from a completely different time zone.

Most of the popular vacation rental websites all include availability calendars and usually you can sync them up to your website. But if you are just starting and not paying to be on these sites, you can easily download a calendar for free.

Step 2 (confirming dates), is when I can inform them of all the requirements on my end. They are able at this point to review the rental agreement and deposit information. Again, this alleviates much conversation as all details of the unit along with the rental rules are spelled out clearly. I have had several people tell me that the professionalism of this agreement is what made them feel comfortable booking my rental.

In Step 3 (booking deposit payment), by now there have been a few emails back and forth (using my form letters in Chapter 6 to save time) with the guest. This kind of gradual communication has now created a bit of a relationship, and not overwhelmed them with too much information all at once. They are comfortable at

---

[3] - See resource section for sites providing calendars to upload to your site.

this point to call or email to secure the reservation with their deposit on their credit card.

Again, the point is to make this *easy* for them. I once called to ask about a vacation rental in the mountains, and the woman who picked up the phone actually told me she **DIDN'T KNOW** how to take my reservation. She explained they just started their rental and hadn't figured that part out yet! She said she would ask her husband and get back to me. I hope you guessed that I didn't stay with them. I can't imagine anyone wanting to be the guinea pig for people who aren't prepared.

If you do not sound confident, and the communication with you isn't easy, *most people won't go through with reserving your place*. When it comes to making a reservation online for travel, professionalism is key and opportunity is best served with preparedness!

And lastly, we prominently include our contact information. Potential guests have to be able to reach you. We list only an e-mail address on our site. Most communication until the point of exchanging money is done via e-mail. This is the easiest way and I really utilize my form letters for most questions asked until someone wants to make a deposit.

But it is imperative to respond to initial email inquiries within one hour. To put the potential customer at ease, it's a good idea to have an automated response at first contact that is very personal and warm and states that they will be contacted soon. Remember, many people will be shopping around with other rentals, so you want to get a jump on their first inquiry.

Creating a web site with so much detail is not only for the purpose of showing potential guests what you are offering, it is the absolute grist for the search engine mill. It is what will get your site noticed in cyberspace.

If you are not technically skilled enough to handle this task, you will want to find someone to do it for you. It's easy enough to find a high school or college kid for this help, as some of them are as proficient as the professionals you would have to pay top dollar to hire. You can put an ad on Craigslist or check out Elance to find someone.

Apart from the regular maintenance of Craigslist and recommended vacation rental site memberships, here are a few things that I do to make my site rise in the Google rankings, attracting lots of visitors from a wide number of sources:

1) **Create your site as a blog** – even though it isn't one.

Sites that are constructed as a blog are 1000 times more visible to search engines. The search engines get pinged every single time there is any activity on the site such as adding pages, photos, comments, etc. The best tool for creating a "blog" site is Wordpress. It's a free of charge software that is provided by your site hosting service. Wordpress is easily configurable, expandable, and customizable. It has hundreds of valuable free plug-ins such as photo galleries, customer management tools, calendars, coupons, online payment tools, databases, etc. It even has a podcast (Internet radio) plug-in.

2) **Make the site rich in text.**

There should be a great deal of text relating to your business, on every single web page. Everyone won't necessarily read *all* text, but you need to have it. Search engines look for words—words and more words! You don't have to write gibberish, just lots of text related to your rental, location, activities located near your place...anything pertinent. You can even have thousands of words of content by placing it at the very bottom of each page and then changing the text color to match the background so it becomes invisible.

3) **Use great titles on your web pages**.

When you go to a page on the web, the browser window has the page's title at the top. That title is a major player in the search engines. Every title in your site should be chock full of the **MOST** pertinent info about your rental. The more web pages in your site, the more "meat" there is for the engines to grab onto. So I create all kinds of "helpful" pages that are totally unnecessary and I have very demure links to them throughout the site.

4) **Make lots of folders.**

After you have all these "helpful" web pages, put them in lots of folders within the backend of the site named stuff like "bestlittlehotelintown" and the name of your town such as "losangeles." Almost everybody puts all their images in a folder called "images". But that folder could actually be called "bestlodgingdealintown". Think of what the search engine would be seeing. "Images" means nothing to the search engine but lodging in the name of your town does.

5) **Name all files with pertinent names.**

This is a really major step to getting recognized by the search engines.

Almost everybody names files like this:

MyCompanyLogo.jpg

Editorial.jpg

mainpage.htm

secondpage.html

cute_model.jpg

biography.html

rates.jpg

rates.htm

contact_us.jpg

contact_us.htm

etc.

So the person trying to find your rental is looking for "lodging" and "accommodations" and the search engine scans your site and finds "MyCompanyLogo.jpg" and then moves on because your images and files have nothing to do with the search criteria.

However, if the search engine came across your site with the following files, it would think it hit the jackpot:

lodgingandaccommodations.jpg

cheapestmotels.jpg

vacationrentalsincalifornia.htm (or whatever city and state you are in)

californiamotelsandhotels.html (or whatever city and state you are in)

[yourcity]lodging.jpg

discounthotelsandmotels.jpg

etc.

Also, keep your files several folders deep with related names. So, you might have a folder called "cheapestcalifornialodging". When the search engine loads the actual page, it will look like this:

http://www.YourCompany.com/cheapestcalifornialodging/lodgingandaccommodations.jpg

You see, it's **RICH** in good search terms at every level. Making files and folders with these non-intuitive names is a real hassle and a half to layout and work with, so I personally keep a little legend that tells what the real files are named.

## 6) **Push your own site!**

One of Google's main criteria for ranking sites is how many sites are linking back to it. The more sites that point to your site, the more Google thinks your site is valuable.

Here is a list of promotional ideas you can implement to get your site out there:

a) Go to every single related directory on the web and add your listing (or hire a teenager to do it for you).

b) Visit related blogs and message boards all over the place and surreptitiously drop in your site url within the context of a comment.

c) Only submit your site to the search engines once per 4-6 months.

d) Start Social Networking (Youtube, Facebook, Twitter, LinkedIn etc.)

Social networking is imperative for publicizing your product or brand. You should utilize as many of these tools as you can manage. Get your rental a Facebook page pronto. Get people following you on Twitter, "tweet" about things happening in your city, great reviews people gave you, new restaurant openings...anything. Offer Facebook specials and ask all your friends to pass your name on! Offer a Facebook discount if a potential guest "likes" your rental page. These social networking venues are the best way for you build an ongoing relationship with your guests. It may be worth it to hire or barter services with a social media expert for one solid week to launch your business. I barter services for time in my rental all the time.

e) Make little video clips of your place and post them on Youtube.com with lots of pertinent key words (known as "tags"). Post a new video anytime you can that shows different features about your place. Make sure the video is really professional and that your place is well represented. Once the video is made, put in on all video clip sites that complete with Youtube.

f) Plug your place frequently with a link/photos on all social media. Offer special deals when you have an imminent vacancy.

g) Start a podcast (Internet radio series) about your place or the immediate town and vicinity. Make sure the podcasts is originating on your main site and put links to your site on each episode.

h) Appear as a guest on real estate, entrepreneurial, and travel podcasts. One angle to discuss could be the secret ins-and-outs of your city. Whenever you have an audience, plug your website as often as possible.

i) Email all your friends and colleagues to let them know about your place.

j) Offer a "one night free" gift certificate to local fund raising auctions. For example, schools often have auctions of small business services as a means of raising money. By offering up your place, you are getting lots of free advertising that will more than cover the cost of the donated booking you provided. We have offered one free night on such auctions, and usually people want to stay for two, so they end up paying for one.

k) Find a publicist to barter with who can help get articles about you in various travel magazines. An article carries much more clout than a paid ad.

l) List your website, on local church, hospital, and community online and physical bulletin boards. People are always needing a nearby and affordable place to park their relatives for family gatherings (weddings, new baby, hospital visits etc.).

m) Contact local tour and excursion businesses to let them know about your place for their customers. It helps them book tours when their clients have an convenient place to stay. They can link your website to theirs and maybe even give coupons for your place.

n) Once you have some money to spend to list your property on vacation rental sites like VRBO, HomeAway, etc., make sure that you include the **maximum** allowable text in each field of the forms you are using during set up and make sure that text is loaded with key words that represent your place.

# CRAIGSLIST & YOUR WEB SITE

How to maintain your presence!

Even though it has lost a lot of its punch due to over saturation of irrelevant postings, Craigslist is still an immediate, powerful, and FREE marketing tool that can attract customers to your property within minutes. Remeber that airbnb.com uses it to get your rental out there, and that speaks volumes of the power of Craigslist. Here are a couple important tips about posting your property on Craigslist.

1) Include your link in the very first sentence of the posting. Once the ad has expired, browsers like Google will still show the first line of text from the ad in the search results. So you want your prime info in the first line. (Example: "Los Angeles Vacation Rental $100/night - http://www.yourproperty.com). Note that it is ok to throw syntax and grammar to the wind in order to get the important stuff in the first line. This ain't Shakespeare, it's cold marketing.

2) Only post your ad every 3 days. If you do it more, your ad will be "flagged" (deleted) for over-posting.

3) Always include at least one photo in the ad. Also, include a few HTML photos that link to your site by inserting the following command in your ad:

<img
src"=http://www.yourwebsite/yourimage.jpg">

This HTML photo tool is great for the search engines because the HTML photos have direct links to your site, instead of just having a generic Craigslist photo.

4) Hone your ad and put as many geographically specific words and key words as you can. Mention your city, neighborhoods, state, landmarks, etc. Make sure to use the key words in actual sentences, not just a list.

5) Never post your ad in the wrong city or area. Your ad will be flagged and dumped. When we first started listing on Craigslist, we thought it was a good idea to let the people in New York know that our place was available in California. So we posted on the New York Craigslist. The ad got black listed (which is worse than being flagged). So don't even go there. Besides, if a New Yorker wants to travel to California, they will be checking the California Craigslist for vacation rentals.

6) Don't get additional email addresses and try to post your ad as a different Craigslist user. Your real ad will be flagged and dumped.

7) Always, include the cross streets for the Google or Yahoo Maps choice in Craigslist.

8) List all your amenities! Many Craigslist users search by the amenities.

9) Once you have honed your ad to the point where it works well and doesn't get flagged, don't mess with it. Just renew the post every three days.

And finally, it's really important to take the scam warnings from Craiglsist seriously. When you click any category searching on Craigslist, there are warning links. Read them and stay current on these because scammers become more and more sophisticated and the scams keep evolving. I have been approached by a few very clever scammers and almost fell for a popular scam once...but only once! You can read all about it in Chapter 8.

### ADVERTISING ON VACATION RENTAL WEBSITES

You may have noticed that at the bottom of my ad I also include my property listing on a vacation rental site that I advertise on called homeaway.com. If you don't know about homeaway.com yet, it is a site where travelers go to find rentals.

There are *many* of these sites where you can list your property. Most of them charge a pretty hefty fee, but when you start making money...some of them are totally worth it. For instance, homeaway.com costs approximately $350.00 per year to advertise. I only did this **AFTER** I started making money from using free Craigslist ads. Shop around on these sites and find which one(s) would work best for you. One way to do this is to compare how many listings in your area each site has, and start with the one that has the fewer listings competing with you.

96

I happen to like homeaway.com and have always gotten top-level guests from that site. I currently use homeaway.com, airbnb.com and Craigslist, and have plenty of traffic from those three sources, in addition to my repeat customers.

I point people from my Craigslist ad to my homeaway.com site, where they can see my current availability calendar and all details of my rental. With the homeaway.com site, I only need one solid booking of four nights to pay for my annual service with them, and then they don't take any other fees. You can usually synch up your availability calendar on any site that you end up using. Make sure it always synchs up with your web pages, so everything stays consistent.

A partial list of some popular vacation rental websites out there now are:

**Airbnb.com**

**Homeaway.com**

**VRBO.com**

**1Villa.net**

**FlipKey.com**

**Vacation Rental Direct.com**

**Villa4Vacation.com**

**Omgtravel.org**

Obviously the more places people can learn about your rental, the better odds at consistent bookings. Many of these sites offer tips on operating and maximizing your rental, but just beware that many of the tips require you to *pay extra*. These sites will also try to sell you "tools" that can enhance your bookings. Those can include ways for them to collect money on your behalf, special protection against loss, etc. You just have to realize they are a business and putting their interests first. Many of the "tools" they offer can be implemented on your own. Please be aware that many of them focus on "destination" rentals and not so much city rentals.

Homeaway.com produces an annual trade show for owners of vacation rentals that is quite large and seems impressive. I have never had the need to go to one, and really see these "trade shows" as a way for them to sell you more. They have plenty of companies joining them, such as security companies with people convincing you need to buy their brand of locks, alarms and what not's. I really don't think this is necessary unless you are investing in multiple second property locations and want information on that type of set up.

When you are researching which websites for advertising you may want to use for your rental, be very sure of what they do and if you are comfortable with all aspects of their service. For example airbnb.com requires that all payment between you and your guests go through them. I personally am not thrilled with that idea, but I use them anyway. They also do not require a rental agreement when people book through them, but you can insist on a rental agreement as a requirement of your rental anyway.

98

# CHAPTER 6

## Securing a reservation

---

*"To give real service you must add something which cannot be bought or measured with money, and that is sincerity and integrity."* - DONALD A. ADAMS

---

When I began my rental business, I spent a couple of months digging deep into all of the different people, situations, price structures, and details that were listed on Craigslist as well as other vacation rental web sites.

The number one mistake being made out there, in terms of hooking potential guests, was the way people were **communicating** what they had to offer. It seemed the easiest thing to me, but I have a background in restaurant management and have experience with the concept of customer service.

I was amazed at how many people seemed to either not know the answers to the simplest questions I posed, or really care about hooking me as a customer. If you can't hook me right away, I will go elsewhere. If it isn't easy for me to understand what you are selling and to have some kind of positive emotional feeling when I first have contact with you, I will move on. "Moving on" is a simple mouse click away for anyone to the next search result (your competitors) listed. I'll bet more people feel this way than not.

Many people I spoke with left me with more questions than I originally called about! They had a good idea, but just didn't see the details through. There are just too many choices out there in our instant "got to have it now" society whether I'm buying a burger or a new car! You must remember most people will want the level of ease that they would get at a hotel.

And yes, many people I contacted had it together and I am not inventing anything new here, but I recognize the value of customer service and satisfaction. My main goal here is tell you that the most important key to getting someone to make a reservation at your place is to be **prepared**, **warm**, **friendly** and **confident** about what your service is. Anticipate the questions they will want answered and make them feel welcomed. By the way, be sure to put these questions in the FAQ section on your site. It may be a bit tempting to get defensive at times with some questions because this is your home, or at least a space you created, but you have to remember this is a business. Remember, the guy in Canada got so defensive, that he lost us as customers.

Before you can begin and have your actual first experience with having guests arrive, you will need to decide some important policies and have them communicated on your site and in form letters (see form letter # 1).

Will you have a separate cleaning fee? Many people do and I do not. Most guests are happy that I don't. Will you collect a separate

100

tax? I include the tax in the total rate and make sure I report my income from my rental. What will your deposit amount be? I charge $100 for any reservation under 7 nights and ½ of the total amount of the reservation for any booking over 7 nights. (all spelled out clearly in my rental agreement). How many people will you allow in your rental?

The occupancy topic alone is very important. Just last week, I had an inquiry of someone who wanted to come for one month with two kids ages 7 and 10.... *and* she wanted a discount. I wrote her back and said we have a maximum occupancy of just two. The woman then tried to change my mind explaining that they were all very neat and quiet.

Now I want a month long booking as much as anyone, but this was a big red flag to me. Our web site states that we have a maximum occupancy of two persons only, and I confirmed that with an email. So she already was trying to talk me into something I cannot give her. She was asking for a special discount because her kids were young, (it's fine for people to ask, and to sometimes grant discounts depending on how busy you are). I didn't want that booking because of this next story.

Way back before I knew better, I used to have a fold out futon sofa in the little sitting area where I now have a loveseat. Well, one woman booked in who told me she would be coming with her daughter and the one bed would be fine.

When she showed up, we just saw her and the one daughter, but the next day we saw her plus *three* kids leaving the rental. This was tricky because I couldn't very well ask her if they all had spent the night. Maybe the others were just visiting, but I had a feeling that wasn't the case. After they left at the end of their stay, I went in to clean. What a mess I found. They had shopped and left shopping bags, receipts, empty cosmetic boxes and all kinds of trash sitting around. But the biggest violation was that they got into my linen cabinet (before I had a lock on it), folded out the futon and made another bed! It took me three times as long to clean the place and wash the linens! Had I been using a linen service at that time or paying a cleaning person, that would have equated to three times the money I had to spend, and since my rates were pretty low back then, so it would have been like giving the room away.

It was very clear to me that they all had stayed there. This is the experience that prompted me to add a provision in my rental agreement that could have allowed me to automatically charge their credit card for the excess mess and the obvious two extra people who slept there. This experience also made me see the importance of keeping my linens locked in a closet. They are also not welcome to come back. Ever.

I cannot stress how important it is to be very clear about how many people are allowed in your rental.

Of course these decisions are all up to you. You can check around and see different listings of rentals and learn what other people do and decide from my input and some other ideas. You don't have to wait to be in a situation similar to the one I just described.

Make sure you have as many questions answered on your website that you can possibly anticipate. Once you activate any Craigslist ad, or vacation rental website listing, be *prepared* for travelers from all over the world to find *you*, because they are out there looking! Do your best to ensure that they choose your place.

### SO HERE IS HOW IT ALL STARTS WITH A POTENTIAL GUEST:

A guest finds our listing from one of our advertising and marketing sources that we use, and from that ad they are directed to view our web site for details, if they haven't already done so.

Most people actually do really view the site thoroughly, but some people do not take the time to read even the basic details of a site right away and they mass email their query to many rental owners at once.

Regardless of whether they saw the website or not, they usually email asking about availability, I do not list my phone number on my web site. My initial contact with anyone is through email. Many people do list their phone numbers on their rental websites, but I do not. Although I love talking one on one with the guests and always use that time to develop a relationship with them, I only want people calling me who are securing a reservation with their credit card.

This cuts down on any "looky loo's or anyone just shopping for information, which saves my precious time. Of course, once someone is booked in and actually staying in my rental, I am always available by phone during regular business hours, unless there is an emergency (I have never had one in 6 years). Because our set up is so well thought out and our transactions so automatic, I rarely get any calls.

It's important to be able to respond as quickly as possible to any inquiry. My research has shown that you will have a better chance of securing the reservation if you respond to an inquiry within three hours. The best way to do this is to have your smart phone notify you when you get any new email. Otherwise, if you have the time, you can list your telephone number and have them call direct. The point is to be available in whatever way works for you. I work at home and am near my computer most of the day, so I can see emails constantly, I simply count on my smart phone when I am away from home.

By the time they are ready to book a reservation, we have emailed a few times, and that is when we usually speak on the phone, unless they are from out of the country and those people usually email the credit card info. The important thing is that we both have a paper trial. I have a credit card number on file for them, they have all my emails and my phone number by this time. We have built a relationship around the transaction. They are emailed a written confirmation with the address and directions for arriving only *after* I receive their signed rental agreement. I don't think you would want just anyone having your address or certainly thinking your rental might be unoccupied.

The best tool I have to help me for all communication with the guests are my form letters. These letters are stored as drafts in my guest house email folder. All I have to do is add the name of the person I am sending to, and hit send. They can be altered for any specific questions, or just sent as general information. These letters are very thorough and can be used from the first communication, to the follow up after they have left your rental. Form letters are the ultimate time savers.

Here are the 8 form letters that I use along with a brief description of their purpose:

---

**Form letter #1**: My initial response from their inquiry from Craigslist, homeaway.com etc. Please note that if you don't accept credit cards, you should insert your PayPal info here. If you do accept personal checks (not recommended) you can put your mailing address in place of my credit card info.

Hello (their name here),

Thanks so much for your interest in our guest bungalow. I hope you have read some of our previous guest reviews to get an idea of how comfortable and popular the bungalow is!

We're happy to let you know that your requested nights are currently available, at the rate of $ (your nightly rate). The cleaning fee and tax are included and there are no other fees.

The first step is for you to make your booking deposit of $ (whatever you require). We change our online calendar and save your dates, only when you make your deposit. The booking deposit is deducted from the total of your reservation. The balance due is charged automatically on your arrival day.

We accept most major credit cards for all payments. You can call us (or leave a message) at (your number) to secure the booking with your credit card —or you can send us your credit card info by EMAIL. Please include:

- Type of card
- Account number
- Address associated with card
- Name on card
- Expiration date
- Security code for the card usually located on the back in the signature block, or on the front of American Express cards.

I have attached our rental agreement here for your review so you know the details. We require the rental agreement to be filled out, signed and sent back to us before we send your confirmation. You may email back or fax to (your fax number if you have one).

Once we receive your signed rental agreement, I then send you a written confirmation of your reservation, balance due, directions for arrival, and entry codes (this is a key-less property).

The bungalow is a very special place with many return guests and we know you will enjoy it. Thanks!

Cheers,

(Your name and number here)

www.yourwebsite

---

You may have noticed that form letter #1 is the first time I give out my telephone number. When it's time to exchange money, then it's time to get on the phone with the guest. Some people have no problem sending their credit card info in an email, but most people want to talk to a live person when it comes to paying for something. The exception to this is most Europeans will email payment info because of the time difference and communication barriers, although most of them speak some level of English.

---

**Form Letter #2:** The actual "order form" that I take down for each reservation, for my records.

# VACATION RENTAL/RESERVATION FORM

Check in date:_____

Check out date:_____

Total nights reserved:_____

Name:_____

Address:_____

City:_____

State & Zip code:_____

Phone number:_____

cell phone:_____

Email:_____

AMEX          VISA          MASTERCARD   (circle one)

Credit                                                    card
number:_____

Expiration date:_____   Security code:_____

Rate per night:_____

Total due:_____

Amount of deposit:_____

Date deposit paid:_____

Balance due upon check in:_____

Date      confirmation     and      entry      codes
sent:_____

Misc. notes:

---

This "order form" gets stapled on top of the front of the signed rental agreement and has all the pertinent info that you would ever need to review all together on the one page. It's also a great place for any follow up notes.

---

**Form letter #3**: Room unavailable for requested reservation dates:

Hello (their name),

Thanks for your interest in our vacation rental. Unfortunately, we are currently booked during your requested dates. I certainly will contact you should we have a cancellation during that period of time.

For future reference, our availability calendar is always accurate at the following site: www.yourwebsite

We hope you will find a time to visit us in the future, and good luck to you!

Cheers,

(Your name)

www.yourwebsite

---

**Form letter #4**: Reservation pending form letter:

Hello (their name),

Thanks so much for your inquiry of our guest bungalow. We do have a reservation pending for that block of time. I am supposed to receive the deposit for that booking within the next two days. If you like, I can follow up with you later and let you know if there is any change.

You can see some pictures and read other details including guest reviews at the following link:

www.yourwebsite

Cheers,

(Your name and number here)

www.yourwebsite

I make it a policy never to actually "hold" a reservation without a deposit. Occasionally while I am waiting for the confirmation of a new inquiry made, I will get another inquiry for the same block of time. Form letter#3 buys me some time to not lose a potential booking. I simply notify the first person telling them that I have another inquiry and let them know I will honor their reservation if they make their deposit within 48 hours. If they can't do so, I give the booking to the second person right away. This happens more during summer months.

**Form letter #5**: The written confirmation form letter with all the details of their reservation.

Hello (their name here),

You are confirmed at NAME OF YOUR PLACE for (insert number of nights) nights beginning on (insert check in date), checking out on (insert check out date) at the rate of $ (insert your nightly rate) per night, for a total of (insert reservation total). Check in time is (insert time) and check out time is (insert time).

The credit card you provided us has been charged the booking fee of $ (insert your deposit fee), which is applied toward the balance of your stay.

Your balance of $(balance due) will be automatically charged the day of your arrival to the same credit card, unless you contact us in advance with an alternative card. The charge will appear on your statement as being paid to (insert the name of your company IF YOU ACCEPT CREDIT CARDS ONLY).

I am attaching the directions for letting yourself in which include the codes you will need to enter the property gate and the code for the bungalow door (the bungalow is a key-less unit). (OR SEND A MAP AND INSTRUCTIONS FOR PICKING UP KEYS OR WHATEVER CHECK IN PROCEDURE YOU ARE USING)
Can you please confirm with me that you received this confirmation with the door codes?

If you have any questions, please do not hesitate to contact me. Thanks!

Cheers,

(Your name and number here)

www.yourwebsite

I never send the confirmation letter until *after* I have received the signed rental agreement. I used to be a bit loose on this, but more times than I was comfortable with, people would be ready to book in, without me having that agreement on file. That's not a good idea at all for so many reasons. The main reason is once they have been given key codes and can arrive, they are not bound by any rules without that rental agreement. Another important reason is they are aware of and have *agreed* to the rules of occupancy.

You will also notice from form letter #5, that I get paid in full the day they arrive. I mention this also in form letter #1 so they understand how the payment works from the very beginning, and are reminded of it again at the time of confirmation. This takes the mystery out of the money stuff and because I collect balance due automatically, they never have to hand a live person their credit card. I usually charge this amount early on the day of their arrival. On occasion someone's card will have expired between the time they make their reservation and they arrive. It's a good idea for you to make sure in advance of their arrival that their expiration date is good through their vacation dates with you. Your order form is a quick way to check this.

---

**Form letter #6**: Our location form letter. People frequently ask our physical location.

Hello (their name),

Thanks so much for your interest in our vacation rental. Regarding your question about our location, for security reasons we don't give the exact address until someone confirms a reservation. The bungalow is located in back of a main house that has tenants that we do not want to disturb. We protect their privacy as well as yours, if you choose to stay with us.

I can tell you the bungalow is located in the exclusive neighborhood of YOUR NEIGHBORHOOD NAME, near the intersection of YOUR INTERSECTIONS OR LADMARKS.

I hope that helps you out. Please feel free to contact me direct if you have any other questions.

(Your name and email)

---

People often ask the exact address of the bungalow, which I do not give them. They usually want to know how far the place is from whomever they may be visiting or a venue nearby. My web site tells the general location and the nearest intersections for their understanding of proximity in the town. I never give the address until their reservation is confirmed, and I have their rental agreement and credit card on file.

**Form letter #7**: Follow up form letter:

> Hello (their name),
>
> We hope you enjoyed your recent visit and were comfortable at (the name of your place).
>
> We are always looking for ways to improve, so if you have any suggestions for us, we welcome your feedback.
>
> Take care and we hope you will stay with us again in the future.
>
> Cheers,
>
> (Your name and number)
>
> www.yourwebsite

---

You can continue making your guests feel special by sending the follow up form letter #7 a day or so after their visit. They love to have a follow up with you and it makes their departure more complete for both of you. It's an invitation to hear their feedback and another chance to keep them thinking about you!

*After* I get a positive response from form letter #7, I then send letter #8:

---

**Form letter 8**: Review my rental form letter:

Hello (their name),

Thanks so much for your response! We're so happy that you enjoyed our rental!

If you could take a couple of minutes and can go to the following link and write a short review, it helps us tremendously in our (name of rental site you advertise on) rankings!
http://www.vacationrentalcompany's/reviews/page
We really appreciate your feedback!

Cheers,

(Your name and number)

www.yourwebsite

---

If you are using any vacation rental site where you can post reviews, it's a great idea to include the direct link to the page they can write a review for you. I get many reviews simply because I ask for them.

I have on occasion dealt with people who are not computer savvy and ask for directions from the airport, or to the bungalow. For whatever reason they can't find online directions or they don't travel with a GPS. It's a good idea to keep form letters with directions from any airports near you that they would be using and have those directions ready to go with a click of your mouse. Any time and trouble you can save your guests keeps them happy. Happy guests are repeat customers.

## Can we have a look at your place?

People will contact you wanting a friend or relative to stop by and preview your place to see if it's a good fit. If you can accommodate these requests, it's a good idea for a few reasons. First of all, many people are very impressed when they actually see a place in person rather just photos.

Usually whoever comes to view your place will be very honest and let the person inquiring know whether the set up will work for them or not. Typically showing your place is the best way to secure a booking as it offers a lot of reassurance. This is great because you don't want people arriving from far away only to say they expected something different.

Since I moved off site, I arrange all showings just as my cleaning manager is finishing up turning the room around, because she is there and everything looks just as it should when a guest arrives.

The following story is an example of a booking from someone who sent her daughter to see my place *and* it was also a multiple inquiry at the same time. The dilemma of multiple inquiries for the same block of time does happen from time to time (often for holidays). These can be tricky situations.

Maureen called last month wanting to have a peek at our bungalow for her mother coming to visit for one month from Ireland. My favorite kind of guest is someone's mother and or father!

However, in between the time that Maureen called for an appointment to see my place and the actual day of the appointment (3 days later) I had two other viable inquires for some of her mother's block of time.

What to do? I have a strict policy of never blocking dates for anyone without a deposit, so my calendar displayed availability to anyone viewing it since nobody had made a deposit but had only inquired. Maureen's booking was for a full month while the others that inquired were for a total of eleven days combined. There was over $1,000.00 more to be made from Maureen's booking. Naturally, I really wanted her booking.

I called Maureen letting her know that others were now inquiring about her mother's block of time. I certainly didn't want to pressure her, but I told her I couldn't hold a reservation based only on an inquiry. I suggested it would be a good idea for her to see the unit sooner than planned, if that was possible. Maureen agreed to an earlier appointment the next day.

In the meantime, I told the others inquiring that I did have a reservation *pending*, and was waiting for the deposit. I told them I would get back to them within 48 hours with the status. I didn't really *have* a pending reservation; I just had to be willing to bet that Maureen would actually reserve when she saw the unit. And if she didn't, there were two different reservations standing by. These are the times I wish I had a duplex in the same neighborhood to handle the concurrent bookings!

Maureen was very impressed when she arrived the next day to view the property, and did, in fact, secure her mother's reservation on the spot. I immediately contacted the others interested to let them know. It's important to make a connection with them even while turning them away. After this connection is established, a large percentage of them will try our place on another visit. It's also great to tell them you will keep their info on hand in case of a cancellation.

You will experience some people who make an inquiry, come and see the rental, say they love it, and do not end up making a reservation. I always follow up directly with them and ask them outright if there was something they didn't like. Their answer usually has nothing to do with me personally or the unit I am offering. Sometimes it's because they like another rental's location, or would like a bathtub (I have a large nice shower but no tub), be closer to the mall, or any number of reasons that still don't diminish my rental.

## All About Payments

One thing I realized after a full year of operating my rental was that I could *get paid in full before they arrive!* This finally occurred to me after one too many times of not being home when guests would arrive. It was always really awkward to try to track people down and I didn't want to seem like a pain or like I was

119

watching their coming and going activity, but it's important to get paid and know that all is well once someone has arrived.

People are accustomed to paying *upon check-out* at a hotel, since that is how hotels work. But if you train them from the start (Form letter #1), which explains how the payment schedule works in your vacation rental, they are fine with it. And you won't ever have to waste your time trying to get your money.

Another important point about collecting your money in full *before* they arrive is, if by chance there is a problem with the credit card for the balance due, you have time to call their cell phone number immediately to let them know and take care of any glitch before they check in. As stated earlier, I run all final guest charges *early* the morning of a guests arrival and have plenty of time to reach them before the check in time of 3PM.

On a few occasions I have had credit card charges that were declined. It's usually because of a expiration date issue with the card but there are various reasons whey the original card used for the booking deposit may no longer be valid.

I have *never* had a guest that did not immediately take care of any problem. But if I ever do, I simply could send my cleaning woman over to change the entry code they were assigned and that guest would not be able to enter the unit unless they contacted me. Like I said, I have never done this and my policy of collecting upfront has been problem free.

Let's cover personal checks.The first thing I can say about this is that you have little to no recourse if a check bounces. I learned this from another home business I used to have. I once accepted a check from another state, the check was no good and the person was long gone…after I had sent my product to him. I was stuck. I couldn't very well fly to that state and try to take him to court. Never again. Most people traveling have credit cards.

I once stayed at a vacation rental in Northern California and the woman running it accepted checks only. I sent her my deposit check and all was well. She did not live on the property of her rental and when we arrived she had left a note on the door saying she would stop by *the next morning* to pick up another check for the balance due.

Well, I could have been long gone by then. I wasn't of course, but what happened was that we were not on her schedule! We missed her for about a day and a half. She would come by and leave notes. Not very smart, convenient or professional. And of course by the time her bank cleared my check once she got ahold of me, I could have written a bad check (of course this is just an example of a what if) and she might have been totally out of luck with getting paid.

The one time I did accept a check was with our very first guest, (Amy who is mentioned in the Almost Horror story section of the book). Big mistake since I wasn't able to automatically charge her for the big mess she left me. Once again, the problem with accepting any checks are that by the time that check clears your bank, the person is long gone. And then there are the obvious fraud issues.

I accept credit cards *ONLY*. The paper trail of a credit card makes me feel very comfortable, and it makes my guests feel comfortable as well. I have never experienced a credit card dispute from my rental business, but I have disputed two charges for vacations I have taken, one from a hotel and one from a B& B. Credit card disputes are no fun, but I did not get what was promised at these establishments and the credit card company sided with me both times. It took a long time, but having some recourse is a good thing.

If you have a smart phone and live on site, you can get a scanning device for credit cards that will scan a card and put the money right into your bank account (see squareup.com). This is the best way to go. Or if you have any kind of a retail business, your credit card merchant can set you up with an additonal terminal and you can receive payments into your business account.

I also don't accept any cash. I did from time to in the first year of being in business, but I found that I didn't like the questions that came up in my mind about these people paying cash. Each time someone paid me cash, and there was no paper trail besides my rental agreement, I got very uncomfortable. If they damaged something, I had absolutely no way to be paid. I would never even see any damage until *after* they checked out. Besides that, accepting credit cards legitimizes you to your guests.

On occasion, people do not have a credit card. I invite them to use PayPal and I always ask the guest to pay the percentage I am charged from PayPal for the transaction. You can go to PayPal.com and set up an account with them and research how that all works. PayPal is a solid alternative to not accepting credit card payments.

I am not an accountant and I certainly am not giving any advice here, but it's my opinion that you should *ALWAYS* report all of your income. Credit card payments make detailed accounting for taxes very easy. Cash does not.

Always get paid in full before guests arrive. It's easier and cleaner for everyone.

# CHAPTER 7

The Rental Agreement: The holy grail of protection for you and your guests.

---

*"Quality in a service or product is not what you put into it. It is what the client or customer gets out of it."* - PETER DRUCKER

---

## PROTECT YOURSELF WITH A RENTAL AGREEMENT and INSURANCE

In my opinion, it is absolutely crucial that you have two things firmly in place before you ever let someone rent from you. Those are insurance and a rental agreement. The rental agreement clearly states what is provided in the unit along with all rules, guidelines, liability terms and conditions. Everyone should know upfront what to expect with situations such as any property or personal damage.

The rental agreement can be suited to your specific set up and needs. It's best to consider your insurance coverage terms, while designing your agreement. For example, when we opened our vacation rental, we allowed access to a hot tub on our premises. On another part of our property we had a free standing small above ground small pool in the summer (it seems it's always summer in Los Angeles) and although the guests were not invited to use the pool, they were invited to use the hot tub during certain hours.

I just assumed that my homeowners coverage would cover me for any liability claim, but I decided to call just to verify and tell them what I was doing. I was quite surprised to learn that although my rental unit was legally permitted, I would only be covered for insurance with a permanent tenant. If I was accomodating a stream of transient people (short term renters), I had *no coverage* at all. Gulp.

I thought this new information would put an end to my rental business right then and there. But, when I asked my insurance representative if they had any ideas, they suggested I contact a company (James Wolf Insurance) that writes Bed & Breakfast and small hotel insurance policies. I assumed that kind of coverage would be cost prohibitive, but I was wrong. It's actually quite affordable.

The premium for top coverage on my bungalow averages about $85 per month. That is approximately the price for one night in my rental. That is the best $85 I spend all month, as it gives me complete peace of mind, should I ever have an injury, fire or any other unforeseeable emergency in my rental.

When the new insurance rep came out to view the property, I was told that as long as a guest had *any* access to my hot tub or tiny pool, I would be responsible for any kind of accident. I immediately removed the invitation of using the hot tub out of the

126

rental agreement, and I had tall fences put in to divide the pool access from the bungalow. The last thing anyone needs here is any worry about a child falling into a pool, or any other safety concern that could be devastating to either party involved.

Liability is addressed in item #18 in the following rental agreement I have included. You just want to be sure that any guest understands exactly what their limitations are and that they have signed an agreement  stating this understanding. You can customize your agreement to be specific to your property and your level of ease regarding all boundaries of the rental you offer.

One great reason for using airbnb.com is that they provide what they call a "Host Guarantee", which covers many possible losses for owners. This host coverage is spelled out in detail  on their website and their agents are easy to reach to get more info on this. You might want to read up on this feature if you decide to use them because this can put your mind at ease should you be worried about the issue of liability and loss. It's a pretty extraordinary service they offer for free.

A key feature of using a rental agreement designed by you is it spells out the specific house rules whether you are renting a room under your own roof, a separate converted garage, guest cottage, pool house or any other set up. People will have a clear understanding of how it works, what happens if they cancel their reservation, throw a wild party, make an excessive mess or damage your property. Honestly, since requiring a rental agreement, I have never once had a situation that was out of control.

I have had a few excessive messes (which I charged and got paid extra for), but each time I explained the situation to the guilty party, the tenant usually had an excuse that they were in a hurry to catch a plane or something like that. They were quite honestly embarrassed as they know they left a mess, so they aren't surprised when I have to charge them. It's best to call them *direct* immediately upon discovering anything out of place or against the policy they agreed to.

You can scour the Internet to search out an agreement, ask for different rental agreements from competitors, or since I have already done that for you, you can just use this one that I created:

# SHORT TERM RENTAL AGREEMENT

Name of your rental

Your telephone number (from 9:00AM – 8:00PM Pacific time)

Please call 911 for any emergency.

TENANT VACATION RENTAL AGREEMENT

(Please sign and return)

----------------------------------------------

TENTANT NAME:

----------------------------------------------

TENANT ADDRESS (Include City, State, Zip):

----------------------------------------------

TENANT HOME PHONE:_____

CELL PHONE:_____

----------------------------------------------

DRIVER'S LICENSE OR PASSPORT NUMBER (include State or Province)

UNIT BEING RESERVED:

1 Bedroom Studio Guesthouse for double occupancy

RESERVED DATES:

CHECK IN:_____

CHECKOUT:_____

TOTAL NUMBER OF NIGHTS RESERVED_____

NUMBER OF ADULTS_____;
CHILDREN_____;

NO PETS - NO SMOKING

AGREEMENT: (YOUR NAME), and TENTANT agree as follows:

1) Above Tenant is an adult and will be an occupant of the unit during the entire reserved period. Other occupants will be family members, friends or responsible adults. Use of the premises will be denied to persons not falling within the foregoing categories, and as a result they would have to vacate the property immediately without any refund. Door codes (or keys) are only issued to tenant listed herein.

2) NO PETS: No pets are allowed on the premises at any time.

3) EXCESSIVE NOISE Any complaints from neighbors regarding excessive noise or other nuisances may be cause for immediate termination of the lease and forfeiture of the Tenant's payment for stay.

4) SECURITY/BOOKING DEPOSIT: The security/booking deposit is $ (YOUR DEPOSIT

AMOUNT) for rental. The security/booking deposit is due upon making your reservation and will secure your dates on our calendar. The deposit is applied to the total amount of your reserved stay, and upon arrival, Tenant will be automatically charged the balance due, minus the booking deposit.

5) INSPECTION UPON CHECK OUT:

- We are only able to keep our rates low when the bungalow is left the way you found it. If the bungalow requires extra cleaning, we must charge the Tenant a minimum of $40 extra, for additional cleaning time.

- Once tenant vacates the premises, the unit will be inspected and if any real or personal property of the unit is tampered with or damaged the tenant agrees to have his/her credit card charged for all replacements, repairs and excessive cleaning required that is outside normal wear and tear, to restore bungalow to the condition it was rented as.

- PLEASE DO NOT LEAVE ANY UNEATEN FOOD IN THE BUNGALOW.

6) PAYMENT SCHEDULE:

$_____ Rent quoted per night _____Total number of nights booked

$_____ TOTAL RENT for reservation

$_____ SECURITY/BOOKING DEPOSIT (to be paid upon booking reservation)

$_____ Balance due upon check in

(On the day that you are scheduled to arrive, the balance of your reservation will be <u>automatically</u> charged to the same credit card number you provided for the deposit).

7) CANCELLATION: Should you wish to cancel this reservation, notice of cancellation MUST BE IN WRITING AND FAXED OR EMAILED AND CALLED IN TO OUR OFFICE. CANCELLATION MUST BE RECEIVED AT LEAST 15 FULL DAYS PRIOR TO YOUR CHECK IN DATE AND TIME. We will refund the sums you have paid, less a $25 cancellation fee. If your notice of cancellation is RECEIVED LESS THAN 15 DAYS PRIOR TO YOUR CHECK IN DATE, you will forfeit all sums paid, as it is unlikely we can book the space reserved by you.

8) CHECK IN: Check in time is 3:00 PM. EARLY CHECK IN TIMES ARE ALLOWED ONLY WHEN THE PROPERTY IS CLEANED AND READY FOR OCCUPANCY AND PRIOR APPROVAL IS REQUIRED. Check in will not be allowed without the signed rental agreement in the owner's or the owner's representatives, possession.

9) CHECK OUT: Check out time is 11:00 AM. THERE IS AN EXTRA CHARGE FOR LATE CHECK OUT AND PRIOR APPROVAL IS NEEDED. Please leave all remote controls, and other guesthouse property at the location. A $20/ hour fee will be

charged for each hour (or portion thereof) past the required check out time. A $20 per item fee will be charged for each lost remote control or movie (*WE STOCK FREE MOVIES FOR TENANTS ENJOYMENT) in bungalow for Tenant use.

10) CLEANING: The property will be inspected, sanitized and cleaned after your departure. The rental fee you have paid will provide for four hours of normal cleaning so that you can enjoy your vacation up to the last moment. YOU ARE REQUIRED to leave the property in the same general condition that you received it by making sure dishes are done and put away, and the home is generally picked up and ready to be vacuumed, scrubbed, dusted and sanitized. If additional cleaning is required, appropriate charges will be charged to your credit card and you will be notified of the amount, which is based on extra cleaning time and supplies if needed.

11) THERE IS NO TELEPHONE ON THE PREMISES. Please use your cellular phone for communication.

12). WIRELESS INTERNET – The password to login to wireless Internet is located in the black guest services book on the table. The password will be associated with your stay and all Internet activity will be traceable to your login password. Internet access is a complimentary service and the owners do not discount any room rates should Internet service be temporarily down for any reason. PLEASE DO NOT RESET THE INTERNET DEVICE. RESETTING IS SUBJECT TO A $100 FEE (the rate we have to pay to have a tech come to the site). PLEASE CALL US IMMEDIATELY FOR ANY INTERNET PROBLEM, and we will troubleshoot the problem on the phone with you.

13) WHAT WE SUPPLY: The property is equipped and set up as a fully furnished property that will include queen-size bed, bedspreads, linens, blankets, pillows, towels, hair dryer, ironing board, shampoo, soap, coffee, as well as a kitchenette with microwave cooking only, a small refrigerator and an electric toaster. There is also a DVD player with a selection of movies and televisions shows, and basic cable TV (no premium channels). THERE IS NO DAILY LINEN SERVICE.

14) WHAT YOU SHOULD BRING: Plan on packing your personal toiletry items. We are conveniently located across the street from a market should you need additional items.

15) TENANTS LIABILITY: Tenant agrees to accept liability for any damages caused to the property (other than normal wear and tear) by Tenant or Tenant's guests, including, but not limited to, landscaping, misuse of appliances, and/or equipment furnished. If damages are in excess of the security deposit being held, Tenant agrees to reimburse (YOUR NAME) for costs incurred to repair or replace damaged items.

16) NO SMOKING – This is a non-smoking unit. There is absolutely no smoking permitted inside the unit. Smoking is only permitted outside.

Smoking inside the unit is immediate grounds for tenant to vacate the premises and forfeit the entire payment for stay.

17) SLEEPING CAPACITY/DISTURBANCES: Tenants and all other occupants will be required to vacate the premises and forfeit the rental fee and security deposit for any of the following: A.) Occupancy exceeding the sleeping capacity stated on the reservation confirmation. B.) Using the premises for any illegal activity including, but not limited to, the possession, serving or consumption of alcoholic beverages by or to persons less than 21 years of age. C.) Causing damage to the premises rented or to any of the neighboring properties. D.) Any other acts which interferes with neighbors' right to quiet enjoyment of their property, E.) Smoking.

18) HOLD HARMLESS: (YOUR NAME) does not assume any liability for loss, damage or injury to persons or their personal property. Nor will (YOUR NAME) accept liability for any loss or damage caused by weather conditions, natural disasters, acts of God, or other reasons beyond its control, except where such loss, damage or injury results from the negligence of (Your name agents or employees.

19) GUEST HOUSE OF PRIVATE HOME: Although the guest house is private and fenced off from the main house, the Tenant hereby acknowledges the rental unit is on the property of a private home and that the Tenant may experience commonly

expected activity of a private home including but not limited to:

Occupants in the adjacent yard, gardeners (once per week), trash trucks (once per week), standard household activity.

20) ADDITIONAL TERMS AND CONDITIONS: The undersigned, for himself/herself, his/her heirs, assignors, executors, and administrators, fully releases and discharges Owner from any and all claims, demands and causes of action by reason of any injury or whatever nature which has or have occurred, or may occur to the undersigned, or any of his/her guests as a result of, or in connection with the occupancy of the premises and agrees to hold Owner free and harmless of any claim or suit arising there from.

21) PAYMENT IS ACCEPTED IN THE FORM OF CREDIT CARDS ONLY.

*** Please note that there is FREE street parking on (EXPLAIN YOUR PARKING SITUATION HERE). Please read all signs for street cleaning/parking restrictions as Owner does not take responsibility for parking violations.

REMEMBER THAT YOU ARE RENTING A PRIVATE HOME. PLEASE TREAT IT WITH THE SAME RESPECT YOU WOULD LIKE SHOWN TO YOUR OWN HOME.

TENANT
SIGNATURE_____

A note about special conditions in your agreement. It's imperative that you have a condition in your rental agreement stating that if guests make any kind of a "big" mess, that you can charge them an excessive cleaning fee. I had one guest who drank a bit of red wine one night and when I went to inspect the premises the morning she checked out, I found red wine stains all over one wall, part of the carpet and and a towel.

My rental agreement states that there is an automatic minimum fee of $100.00 from any damage caused by a tenant. When I calmly called her to let her know I would be charging this fee, although she was very embarrassed, she had no problem with the charge and let me know if there was any further charges to please let her know. I took many pictures to the document the damage just in case there was any kind of a dispute with her. She claimed she had to check out early to catch a plane, was racing the clock and wasn't aware the damage was so wide spread. The point is, she knew she had signed a document agreeing to that charge, and that she had caused the damage.

It's always a good idea to keep some carpet cleaner on hand (if you have carpets) and some touch up paint. I had both of those items ready and the place cleaned up nicely. I made an extra $100.00 for about 1/2 hour of additional work.

Had someone been checking in right away and the room not been ready because of the damage caused by her, I would have put the arriving guests up in a local hotel and charged that amount to her, with of course a written letter of explanation, a copy of her signed rental agreement, and pictures of the damaged she caused attached to protect myself should she decide to dispute an additional charge on her credit card. I would also include on that letter to her, that I was sending the same package to the credit card company. This would have been an extreme case, but I only have the one place so I really wouldn't have any other option. Luckily nobody was checking in on the day she checked out.

There could be many scenarios here, but I do believe that a detailed rental agreement stating what is expected of people really cuts down on the risk factors of damage. The "red wine" incident" is as bad as I have experienced, and it wasn't really that bad. Just make sure you are covered for something like this. Be sure to think about this or any other particular conditions of your place, and state them in your agreement.

The only other small problem I have encountered is with a couple of people who have left the room needing more cleaning than usual. Specifically, two guys came for three days and left a bunch of food in the sink and in the small refrigerator, as if they were kids away for the first time on Spring Break thinking their mother would clean up after them. In general, they left a big mess. Our kitchenette does not have a garbage disposal and we have a specific small sign stating such, and requesting no food be put down the sink. Well they had all kinds of garbage in the sink. I charged them an additional $25 automatically. They are also not welcome to come back.

My bungalow is much too special and busy to have people treat it that way. This is another good reason to have a MAXIMUM number of people allowed in your place. Imagine if I allowed four people instead of two who were off in pigpen land? If they want to make a big mess, they can go pay hotel prices and stay somewhere else.

Now I did not tell these guys they are not welcome back when I charged them the additional $25, I just told them they left an excessive mess I had to pay my cleaning manager extra. If they ever contact me again to book another reservation, I will gently remind them of the mess they left and I will also tell them that my excessive cleaning fee has been raised to a minimum of $100. I don't need anyone calling a lawyer and invoking violation of The Fair Housing Act (see 9). I doubt they would be interested in paying that much money to be cleaned up after, since one important point of staying in my bungalow is because of the savings.

My rental agreement is a bit different for any booking over 7 nights. I consider this an extended rental, and use the following paragraphs in place of the corresponding paragraphs on the rental agreement included earlier:

4) SECURITY/BOOKING DEPOSIT: The security/booking deposit for  any extended stay is 50% of total amount due for rental. The security/booking  deposit is due upon making your reservation and will secure your dates on our calendar. The deposit is applied to the total amount of your reserved stay, and upon arrival, tenant will be automatically charged the balance due, minus the booking deposit.

7) CANCELLATION: Should you wish to cancel this reservation, notice of cancellation MUST BE IN WRITING AND FAXED OR EMAILED AND CALLED IN TO OUR OFFICE. CANCELLATION MUST BE RECEIVED AT LEAST 1 month prior to your check in date, so we may have the best chance to book the unit. We will refund the sums you have paid, less a $25 cancellation fee. If your notice of cancellation is RECEIVED LESS THAN ONE MONTH PRIOR to your check in date, you will forfeit all sums paid.

It is a much better policy to charge a higher deposit for an extended rental because you will most likely not receive a booking for the same length of time, should someone cancel a booking of over 7 nights.

# CHAPTER 8

## A couple of almost horror stories and what not to do.

---

*"Success does not consist in never making mistakes but in never making the same one a second time"* - *GEORGE BERNARD SHAW*

---

Okay…where do I start here? I guess at the beginning. When we first decided to rent out our bungalow on a short term basis, I put the word out to a few friends. I didn't have a website at this point or advertising of any kind. One of my closest friends, a professional psychotherapist, called telling me she had a client who was in a transition and needed a place for about a month. I should have considered that she was "in transition", but I didn't, and I just thought I was having beginners luck to get my first guest wanting to stay a full month!

My friend assured me her client was responsible and vouched for her. I had a few telephone conversations with this person, Amy, and she sounded just great. She was a young, working student who said she didn't smoke, drink and preferred things quiet.

Amy and I agreed on a price for one month in our bungalow, and I verbally told her the unit was located in my backyard and she would just need to be mindful of the fact that we lived on the premises. I let her know we didn't allow smoking, parties of any kind, excessive noise and we had a small child and his welfare was our biggest concern. Amy assured me that she was seeking a place to just relax and have a quiet time and said we would hardly even notice she was there. My first *big* mistake was we didn't have a rental agreement back then!

So Amy paid half of the month upon arrival, (my second mistake with her was not getting paid in full before she moved in). All was well for a about a week. When early one morning, I mean like 4:00 AM early, my son came in our room and asked who was knocking on the door. My husband and I hadn't heard anything and told him he was just dreaming and to go back to sleep. He came back in again, asking the same question. His room directly faced the bungalow where ours was on the opposite side of the house.

We ventured out into our living room thinking someone was at the door, but then we heard that there was noise coming from the outside in the back at our guest bungalow! My husband went outside and there was a really drunk girl banging frantically on the bungalow door asking Amy to open up!

We were totally shocked and worried, so we asked this inebriated girl to leave immediately or we would call the police. Before she left she mentioned that she was staying there too and had her things in the room. We were shocked as this was a total violation of our agreement with Amy and I was seeing red.

We knocked loudly on the door asking Amy to open up. No answer. We were really concerned so I called Amy's cell phone number...no answer. We decided we should open the door and see what was up. We opened the door and the place was a ***total mess***! Liquor bottles were everywhere and although Amy told us she was a non-smoker, the air was dense with cigarette smoke and there were cigarette butts and ashes in the sink and all over each plate in the kitchenette. The bathroom was even worse with cigarettes and make-up everywhere especially on my new white towels!

That is one reason you never use white towels in a vacation rental for sure!

To top that off, someone had gotten into the storage closet (not locked, which was **our** naïve and trusting nature). Despite an armoire being marked "Personal" Amy had taken a camera that was stored there and had it wired to her computer for God only knows what reason. I have a pretty dark imagination, so of course I went ballistic.

Oh by the way, Amy was nowhere to be seen. I could drag the drama of this out for a few more pages but just to wrap up, we called Amy's cell phone and told her if she wasn't there within a half an hour, we were throwing all of her stuff away (she left a bunch of clothes and linens). We also threatened to call the police on her. In reality, even if we did call the police, they couldn't have done anything because ***we let her into our place***!

Back then we used keys and Amy had one! We had no recourse to keeping her out other than standing guard at 4:30 AM. My husband did this and intercepted Amy and some guy who showed up wearing only a towel (true story) who got there pretty quickly to get her stuff before we tossed it out. We demanded the key back, to which she obliged.

So there are a few crucial points to consider here:

- **ALWAYS** have a credit card number on file for anyone staying, for any possible damages.

- **NEVER** rent to anyone without a signed rental agreement (it keeps out the riff raff).

- **ALWAYS** get paid in full before anyone arrives (we kicked Amy out and I lost out on half of the agreed upon money).

- **ALWAYS** lock up *anything* you do not want others to have access to.

This experience taught me that we did not set ourselves or our rental up professionally. Amy possibly felt because we she was referred by a friend, that our situation would be

more of a casual type of thing. Once we got our website up, a detailed rental agreement was in place and we only accepted credit cards for payment, we never ever had to evict anyone again. Everyone who goes through the channel of a rental agreement takes the rental much more seriously. Even friends who have stayed in my rental, must give me a rental agreement—I mean everyone except our parents and immediate family members.

## The Craigslist Scams

Another thing to absolutely avoid are the Craigslist "money order/cashier check scams! These change frequently, so it's a good idea from time to time to read up on them. Just Google "Popular Craigslist Scams" and you will get all the info you need, as these scammers constantly find new ways to steal.

I fell for one in the beginning. A "doctor" emailed saying he was on a warship in the Persian Gulf and didn't have access to phones, etc. He said he wanted to surprise his nephew with a wedding gift of two weeks in my bungalow, and a really nice bottle of champagne, flowers, candy, and the works. He was sending a "cashiers check" for **_plenty_** of money, and I was to send him a refund for the difference between my actual costs and the amount he sent. I was wary but decided to give him my address to mail the check.

About a week later, I receive a very real looking cashiers check in the mail. Just as I am ready to take it down to my bank—**_another person writes with the exact same message_** being a doctor in the gulf, a wedding gift for his nephew, a refund, blah blah etc! Sure enough, my gut feeling was correct. It usually is.

Obviously the cashier's check (from Canada) was a fake. A bank teller may not have caught that, deposited the funds into my account and I would have cut a check and mailed it to this jerk way before the bank realized the check was no good! By contrast,

145

the funds are always there when using a credit card or PayPal, or the transaction doesn't go through!

I promptly emailed this scam artist "doctor" and told him I was contacting the authorities and turning him in. I was a bit nervous that this idiot had my address, but I have read these people are off shore and just want you to send them money. Never again will I ever fall for one of those scams. They have gotten a bit more clever, but if you hold fast to the rules of credit card payment only, you will avoid these scams.

Be sure to stay up on the Craigslist scams!

And finally let me just mention that I do keep a "Blacklist" of people who are not welcomed back. The reason is because my rental stays very busy and over the course of the past six years I might not remember who made a mess. I can't possibly find the time to sift through all my paper files of people I don't want to deal with, so if I have a problem with someone they go on my list. I am happy to report that there are only three people on this list. One is the guy who made a big mess, one is Amy my very first nightmare guest, and the last is the woman who came with all the kids using the lie that she was only coming with one. Those are pretty great odds considering I have had a couple hundred people come through my rental since I started out.

# *CHAPTER 9*

## Here they come!

*"Act as if what you do makes a difference. It does"- WILLIAM JAMES*

Okay, you have secured the reservation, gotten paid in full (hopefully), and your first guests are on the way! Will you greet them? Will they arrive and have a way to let themselves in if you don't greet them? Will it all be easy and clear to them? What will their first impression be?

If you can make the first impression of you and your place something special and **welcoming,** you will give your guests the feeling that they made the right decision with choosing you, instead of another rental.

If those guests are made to feel special and *save money*, they will come back time and again. I have several guests that stay in my rental on a regular basis. One is a pilot who flies celebrities from coast to coast, relaxing in my rental in between flights. Three or four times a year the parents of a young man in my area call my place their home away from home on their visits from the East Coast. There's the businessman from New Mexico who has been coming once a month for corporate meetings in my area for the past five years! And also two other couples who each try to be first in line to reserve Christmas for the past 4 years!

Now let's think a minute about the time you are willing to give away. There is a lot to be said for standing face to face greeting people coming to stay at your place. Some people love meeting you and feel great about chatting, but the majority of them have just gotten off a plane, driven a long time, waited God knows how long for their bags, picked up their rental car, dealt with all the details of traveling...and could care less about anything you have to say or how cute your kid or cat might be. You must consider these things.

In the early days of my business, I would be very present for all my guests—in the yard or just visible, always asking if people were comfortable. A few times I was invited in to tea or a glass of wine, especially with the Europeans. Although this was quite pleasant —unless you *have the time to socialize,* it might be best to decline. My friend who runs the B&B in his home does make friends with many of his guests. I personally got too busy with my little boy to keep that up for too long.

Now living so far from my rental, all of my socializing with guests is on the phone, email, or we keep up on Facebook. It's much less intrusive for my lifestyle. If you live alone, you might welcome the social aspect of a vacation rental, as the people you will meet are typically very interesting and most definitely very friendly.

It's imperative to make sure your guests' transition into your place is easy. When I first opened my rental business, I made this pretty

148

complicated for myself and probably for my guests as well. I would ask them to give me an estimated time of arrival and I would bust my butt to make sure I was home. I would have them come to the front of my house entering through my gated yard, thinking it was somehow impressive that they had to be "buzzed" through my locked gate!

Well this was all fine and good some of the time, but more times than I care to count, I had a preschooler taking a nap, or we were just sitting down to dinner (the most awkward situation for everyone).

Very often they were arriving at night, occasionally planes got delayed, people got stuck in traffic (especially in L.A.) and the quaint little greeting I planned turned into me sitting there irritated just waiting sometimes for hours! These are not the circumstance to greet anyone who you are hoping will be comfortable.

When situations like any of those happened, I would usually rush through my little "tour" of the property (which really wasn't necessary at all), and just walk them back to the vacation rental. They had their own entrance back then, just as they do now, but I somehow thought everyone would be more comfortable with an initial meeting. That is not true! I would often stand outside while my little boy napped just praying he wouldn't wake up to find me gone and come screaming outside to look for me while I was in the middle of pointing out my prize Gardenia plant with the intention of presenting a relaxed and homey environment!

I finally wised up and realized it isn't necessary that they see my house (or your house if you are renting a detached unit). They

149

don't need a tour of your yard unless there is some space that is common to them that they might actually be hanging out in.

If your rental happens to be a room in your house, **under your roof**, that is an entirely different subject. Just be sure to be clear on what is off limits to them and find a way that makes this most comfortable for you and them. Your rental agreement is a great place for them to learn the physical limits. Maybe restricting their check in and out times to a time of the day where there isn't much activity in your home would be a good idea. If you live alone or with maybe just one other person, this is much easier than if you are raising a family. However if your house is big enough, it may be a non-issue.

Now let's discuss the important subject of money. Back before I figured out that it was much better for everyone concerned to take care of the money **before** they even walked in the door, I used to hold a clipboard with their rental agreement and ask the guest for their credit card when I first greeted them. I would take the card into my house to process it, take it back to them to get their signature. On occasion, the card would be declined and I would have to go knock on their door, while they were just settling in and we would all feel very awkward. My point here is to make sure their arrival is **easy**, unencumbered and *automatic*.

### Oh, the People You'll Meet!

Be assured that you will meet some great people seeking your vacation rental. Here is a list of the most common types of people who frequent my rental:

**The in-laws or parents**: These people are usually in their late 50's or older. They are clean, respectful, and problem free. They have children who live in the city near our rental, but for whatever reason they don't or can't stay with their relatives. Sometimes they just want their own space, and sometime their relatives don't have extra room for them. These people are extremely quiet, clean and respectful.

**The business traveler:** The business traveler is a real asset as they often come back multiple times in one year! As mentioned earlier we have one businessman who comes at least nine months out of the year and he has for the past 5 years. One businesswoman has even recommended my place to others in her firm and we get occasional new people from out of state coming for meetings because of her. The business traveler is really on the go, always alone, uses very little of any supplies and usually tips for housekeeping on their way out. We love the business travelers!

**European couples**: These couples vary from young to old. They are extremely self -sufficient and are accustomed to being in new countries. Many of them smoke, so be sure to make your smoking policy very clear. Most of them like an outdoor space to have access to. They are very Internet savvy so make sure you have a great Internet connection for them because they usually rely on the Internet to take advantage of your entire city has to offer.

**Young adventure seekers:** If yours is a popular city, you will get several young people off alone, sometimes for the first time. I have had my share of worried parents make the reservation on behalf of their kids. For me, as long as the kids are over 18 years old, and I have a valid credit card on file, that is fine with me. I make sure whoever is actually staying in my place actually signs the rental agreement so they know the rules.

Now there is something to pay attention to here about the Fair Housing Act, which reads:

> Title VIII of the Civil Rights Act of 1968 (Fair Housing Act), as amended, prohibits discrimination in the sale, rental, and financing of dwellings, and in other housing-related transactions, based on race, color, national origin, religion, sex, familial status (including children under the age of 18 living with parents or legal custodians, pregnant women, and people securing custody of children under the age of 18), and handicap (disability).

This clearly states the specific things that you cannot discriminate against. However, it does not say anything about age (except for minors with legal custodians), so you can make it your policy not to rent to students or anyone under a certain age. You can clarify this with your local city and state for any legal exclusion about short-term rentals.

You need to convey to your guests that although you may not be visible to them daily (even if you are), that you are at their service for information should they need you. You need to be sure they can reach you if they must. If you set up your place as described, they won't be calling you, but they need to feel like they can.

152

*That's what they are looking for!*

**And finally....a quick little pep talk**

Okay, so you've read my little guide and you might be thinking, "Well, it seems simple enough, but...would I really do this"? Obviously, only you can ultimately answer that question. But, I can tell you that if *I* can do this, you can too.

This isn't rocket science, but I understand as much as anyone the possible resistance of a new learning curve. The transition between thinking about and *actually starting something new* for some people is daunting.

But I promise you that once you get through that first scary hump of "What have I gotten myself into?" and you have successfully accommodated your first guest, you will know how easy this business is. Hopefully you will feel some pride in what you have created and you will really understand the possibility of the income your rental can bring into your life.

Just realize that once you get the initial set up going, you can start right away by simply advertising on Craigslist for free. That is a very easy thing to do, and only ONE task. Of course you then should eventually sign up to list your rental on one of the many vacation rental web sites that will point interested people in your direction. But you can start with just Craigslist and ease into it. With each parting guest you will go more and more on autopilot and move closer to full automation.

Good for you if you are a self -starter. If you aren't, find your support person or persons. Who could that be for you? Mine was and is always my husband. I have been running my rental for a little over six years, but to this day, whenever something comes up that is an unanswered question about my rental and I waiver at all, my husband helps me with the big or little decisions. My rental has become so automatic and reliable; it's rare I have any unanswered questions at all.

If you can operate your rental as a real *business,* and an *opportunity* to present something really special, you have a chance at a real boost in your income, as well as making lots of people very happy that they found you. And 90% of it you can do in your jammies if you like.

To all the naysayers who told me I was crazy to think people would pay to stay in my backyard in the middle of a city, it's six years later. I have so much more financial freedom, I provide a valuable service to many, and…. I have met some really great people along the way. And so can you.

So **BE MY GUEST**… to have fun, prosper, give people what they want and **GOOD LUCK!**

## About the Author:

Pamela Demorest knows first hand that the methods in "Be My Guest… and pay me" can help generate thousands of dollars. For years she has been running a vacation rental in her own backyard in Los Angeles. From a small guest bungalow in the back of her property, she was able to cover the mortgage on the whole property!

Demorest carefully honed her vacation rental operation until it maximized the income and minimized the time and effort required for operation to the point where she could literally move 400 miles away and still run a successful operation.

Ms. Demorest has been successfully operating her Los Angeles vacation rental for over six years. For the past three years, she has managed all operations of her vacation rental remotely–from Northern California in Sonoma County, where she lives with her husband, two sons and dog. Possessing a varied background in both the entertainment and restaurant industries has enabled Ms. Demorest to refine the customer service skills needed to allow a vacation rental owner with any level of experience, the ability to create, market and maintain a thriving vacation rental and achieve an edge over the competition.

Made in the USA
San Bernardino, CA
26 January 2016